MINDSET FOR HEALTH

Using Your Mind to Achieve Your Fitness Goals and Beyond

TDACHI-DENI WHITING

made with love ♥
HECHO CON AMOR♥

MINDSET FOR HEALTH
Using Your Mind to Achieve Your Fitness Goals and Beyond

2021 LeadHer Publishing

Cover Design - Kristie Verdurmen
Interior Design - Christina Williams
Editing - Megan Jackson, Donna Zuniga
ISBN - 978-1-990352-07-2

For more information on the author, visit instagram.com/tdachideni
Facebook: Tdachi Deni-Whiting
Email coachtdachideni@gmail.com

For more information on the publisher, visit lead-her.com
@leadher_inc
Email admin@lead-her.com

Praise for Mindset for Health

"I just want to say how much I truly adore Deni. Her kind heart, great attitude, and desire to help others is truly inspirational! This book is both inspiring and filled with tools to help anyone looking to meet their health goals, succeed!"

—Robert Hollis,
Entrepreneur, Author, Public Speaker,
and documented multimillionaire

"Deni is a true Light Worker in this world! She has done the introspective, hard work herself, and knows of what she speaks, leading by example, walking her talk, consistently and effervescently. She shows up for you from the most authentic and loving of intentions, empowering you with both the mindset and physical nourishment necessary for shifting your lifelong paradigms of less than stellar health management. And most importantly, she kindly gets YOU out of your own way…once and for all! I highly encourage you to gift yourself this book, to dive into safe, supported self-exploration with Deni, to experience her infinite magic. Doing so will transform your life, guaranteed!"

—Julie Thayer,
Yoga Coach, Women's Health & Trauma
Specialist, Kind Movement Expert

"Deni has been an incredible source of light into my life. Reading her take on living a healthy, balanced, mindful life has been an inspiring and motivational experience. Her book is full of perspective shifts, mindset techniques, and real advice you can use to transform yourself into the best possible version of you, however that looks. Making change in your life does not need to be complicated or difficult. Use this book as your sidekick for healthy change and watch how much magic you can create."

—Courtney St Croix,
CEO, LeadHer Publishing, LeadHer Inc.

"The book amazed me because Deni managed to capture one of the most important truths which are to take care of your health through the mind. Throughout my experience in the finance world, I have seen how people seeking their financial freedom, their success, or a promotion at work, lose their health because they do not know how to manage the innate resources in their bodies. In a simple and action-based way, Deni explains the potential of your mind using proven methodologies to help the reader break the paradigms that bind them, leading them to true success with health and money. I recommend that you invest in yourself, use these tools and you will reach levels you have never dreamed of!"

—Consra Rosales,
Executive Partner, New York Life Insurance Company

Dedication

This book is dedicated to those who want to change their health for the better in order to live a healthier and happier life — and for all of you who feel trapped, desperate, and confused about what your health and body are supposed to be like. Health is more than how things appear on the outside. I believe that living a healthy life means being truly connected to both your mind and your body, which in turn allows you to live a happier, more energetic, and more peaceful life.

To my parents, for your unconditional love, support, and for always being my cheerleader in any project (tiny or big) that I choose to do. To my sister, for your unconditional love and support. Lots of this project happened with your help.

This book is also dedicated to all of my friends and family who cheered me on during this process. When you want to accomplish something, you can do it. It doesn't matter what it is. It can be a goal, changing your health, or just following your dreams. You have the power to do it. Just start.

To my son, because you are my motivation and I want to show you the importance of your body and your health. I want to show you that you have to follow your dreams no matter how crazy they may be. To my husband, for always supporting me and my crazy dreams, your love, your patience and for cheering me on to finish this book. You always believe in me. I love you!

To my coach, Kathleen Cameron, for showing me how to open and unleash the power inside of me, and for motivating me to write and finish this book. To my publisher, Courtney St. Croix, because you did such a beautiful job editing and understanding the content of my book. Both of you made this dream come true.

To my clients, for believing in me and for opening your hearts and allowing me to coach you and support you on your health journeys. Every day I wake up with a beautiful feeling in my heart knowing that you are getting healthier and living happier.

—Deni Whiting

Contents

Foreword

When I first met Deni, I knew there was something special about her. She was ambitious and driven, with a passion to help others, and she reminded me a lot of myself. There was an instant connection between us, and I knew that learning to harness her own power was going to change absolutely everything for her. It didn't take long for her to sign up for my coaching program, and she jumped in with both feet.

As a Manifestation & Success Coach who has learned from an incredible lineage of teachers, created an 8 figure business in 18 months and has built a movement helping others create their dream lives, I have seen many people want more out of their lives. However, few will go after it like Deni has.

I still remember the early days when Deni would send me messages. I could tell she was soaking it all in and loving every minute of it. I could feel her soul was lit on fire when she studied herself in relation to the material we both now live by. The truth is, something inside of her attracted in me a longing for more, and I am blessed to have been the one alongside her as she allowed it to come to the surface.

While circumstances in her life made it challenging to stay focused on studying, she made herself the priority. She fought against herself and outside pressures and created so much beauty in her life. She knew her purpose was bigger than what she ever thought possible before and she was stepping into it right before my eyes.

The day Deni asked me if she should write her book, I knew she already knew the answer, she just needed that confirmation. Like so many others, the fear of what others would think, and the voices of judgement looming over us felt all too real. Because she did the work on herself, she was able to replace those voices with her own powerful and confident voice. The doubt she held was moved aside, and her true power came forward in that moment. You see, everything is already within us, all we need to do is allow it to come to the surface. At a young age, we learned many things, and many of those things aim to keep us safe. While I believe the intentions were good, this left us harder on ourselves than needed, and we have become comfortable with the lives we live. While we want more, not many are willing to do the work to make it happen. Our comfort zones feel pretty good, but breaking into the realm of what you once thought was impossible, feels even better.

This is something Deni was willing to do. She was willing to want more and go after it. Her growth has been tremendous and it shows in what she continues to accomplish, including this book, a manifestation brought to life. The principles within this book, if used, will change your entire world. Whether it's health and wellness, relationships, business or gaining more self-love, this book is for you. It is all created within you and from you. It's time for you to harness it all.

What Deni will teach you in this book is priceless. Coming from someone who has applied it to her own life, she is the perfect teacher. As Deni says, "the good news is that you have the solution, and it's already inside you". she teaches you exactly what you need to do to bring the inside out, and be your healthiest, most divine version.

I feel so proud to have read all this incredible knowledge within these pages, and to see how Deni has chosen to use her voice to empower yours.

To your own health and prosperity journey,

Kathleen Cameron
Chief Wealth Creator
CEO & Founder of Diamond Academy

Introduction

First of all, I want to thank you for choosing my book. This book will give you the tools that you need to become the healthiest, happiest person you can be! Lots of people, including myself, have set health goals. Have you ever set a New Year's Resolution? I have, and on New Year's night, it is common for those who set resolutions to be excited because they've decided they will eat healthier, go to the gym, and maybe even purchase a brand new pair of running shoes and cool workout clothes. According to a recent article featured in *Forbes* magazine, every year more than 50% of people make New Year's resolutions, and yet about 80% of New Year's resolutions will get abandoned around the second month of the year.[1] The most common commitments people make are: to exercise more, to improve their diet, and to lose weight. They will start with high hopes, but when they don't see visible results quickly enough, they will quit.

You might blame your boss, your friends, your kids, or the fact that you have no time during the day to work out or eat healthily. The reality is that the only person responsible for not achieving these goals is YOU. Yes, you read that right! Your limited time, your friends, kids, or boss aren't responsible. These are just excuses that you make in your mind, and the only person responsible for what happens inside of your own mind is you. But there's more to it than that. There is something else that stops you from getting the results you want, and it is called a **paradigm.**

If you've never heard of this term before, don't worry. I am going to explain what paradigms are, and how they can control your life and the quality of your health. An easy way to understand paradigms is to think of them like a multitude of habits that you have adopted throughout your life that guide every move you make. They determine the way you live your precious and beau-

---

[1]https://www.forbes.com/sites/jenniferbarrett/2021/01/01/new-years-resolutions-dont-work-try-this-instead/?sh=409e958640db

tiful life. They dictate what you eat, how you talk, your successes, and your failures. You've been developing the paradigms or habits that you currently have since you were born. Your paradigm includes learned and adopted ideas from your parents, your friends, your cousins, your teachers, the television, the radio, social media, coworkers… everything around you. Your paradigms dictate your health and the success that you have when you try to become healthier, eat better, or stick to an exercise plan. If you do not target these habits from your subconscious mind, you will go back to your old habitual behaviours, no matter how good your diet or workouts are.

Don't stress — this problem has a solution, and I will give you the power to solve it throughout this book. By the time we're finished, you will be equipped with the tools and resources necessary to change this paradigm, your thinking, and some additional tools that will help you reach and maintain your goals — and challenge yourself in the future.

There are so many programs, diets, and workouts out there. You can spend thousands of dollars in one year on gym memberships, classes, supplements, and food, but if your mind isn't right, you will never get or keep the results that you want. I am not saying that you will never get results, but there are laws that function in our world that keep us from accomplishing the things that we really want.

I recently discovered the work of an amazing author, Dr. Maxwell Maltz. He wrote a book called *Psycho-Cybernetics* and was the first one to understand and explain how our self-image has the ability to make us achieve or not achieve any goal. Every self-improvement book on the market includes elements of his work. Olympians and athletes are often referred to in this book. What he teaches is what we need to use to achieve any personal goal that we desire. Every single one of us carries a mental blueprint of the beliefs that we have of ourselves. This "self-image" is what makes us believe the person that we are right now. These beliefs or self-images can be changed. Psycho-Cybernetics is simply how our system and mind operate automatically. This is what we are going to be focusing on in this journey. The current habits and beliefs that you have about yourself right now will have to be modified with different exercises that you are going to learn in the next chapters. If you do not change your thoughts, your current experiences, and create a mental picture of what you want, you will gain the weight you lost or never stop eating the food that isn't right for you throughout your life.

So, open your eyes wide and keep reading, because this is going to be so exciting. With this book, you have an opportunity to learn how to change your habits, create a healthier lifestyle, perform better in your workouts, feel confident, energized, and happy, and successfully achieve any fitness goal that you want… if you just apply the steps that I will teach you in this book.

Things Weren't Always This Way for Me

I live a very healthy lifestyle now, and I even teach fitness classes to participants all over the world. I love what I do, and I have made big changes in my life in order to truly create the habits that foster whole-body health, not just weight loss or a certain size. But it wasn't always this way. I had problems with my weight as a child, throughout high school, and into my adult life. As I started learning more about what I could do to change, I read books, asked friends, sought out wonderful mentors, and came to the realization that how we use our minds in every aspect of life is the most important component to get the desired results that we crave. Whether you want to accomplish a fitness goal, a life goal, change your career, make more money, or improve your relationships, everything starts inside of your mind. Our culture has made us think that all of our problems can disappear if we just change the way our bodies look. But it's a vicious cycle when you don't work on what truly matters: your mind. If you don't work on your *mind* first, your habits will not change, you will lose the results you achieve, and you will find yourself back where you started — over and over again. But we're about to change that.

We all have control of our own bodies, our eating habits, and the performance of our workouts. When I began to understand how the mind works, I started realizing how people at my gym, in my exercise groups, and my friends and family created the results they had regarding weight and health. As a population, we have a tendency to say and repeat the wrong messages to ourselves over and over in our minds. It is a repetitive cycle that you cannot get out of if you do not take action. This is one of the reasons I decided to write this book.

As a health coach, I am often asked, "How do you do it?"
How can you say no to that delicious cookie?
How can you eat healthy all the time?
What do you eat or do to perform better in that exercise class?

I am not special in any way. I simply learned how to make my mind work for me, not against me. The thoughts inside your head — the regular "self-talk" that occurs inside your mind, sometimes without you even noticing — can heavily influence the way that you see yourself. This then influences your emotions and feelings, which influences your behaviour, which creates habits, and so on.

You do not need any superpowers to start using your mind to your advantage. It is actually very simple. You just need to discover the knowledge that most of the population doesn't know. You're about to discover how you can capitalize on how your mind works, instead of letting things happen to you and wondering why you aren't able to get what you want. When I learned this information it completely transformed my life, so I feel compelled to share it with the world. I want you to succeed. I want you to feel good in your skin. I want you to accomplish your goals and reach all the results you desire. I was just like you a few years ago. I grew up with a paradigm and unfortunately used ineffective and dangerous ways to appear "healthy." It took me over 30 years to discover this because this knowledge is not common. Your parents, teachers, and friends don't teach or talk to you about this. Your self-image is created by all of your past and present experiences, thoughts, doubts, and beliefs.

The good news is that you have the solution, and it's already inside of you.

The Cultural Relationship To Food

As I mentioned before, I struggled throughout my life with weight management. I was born in Mexico, and I had a beautiful childhood and adolescent experience there until I was 24 years old.

As a child, my mom had the idea that the chubbier I was, the healthier I was. Moms didn't have a lot of information about child health like we do now with the internet. My mom fed me well; I ate the most delicious, satisfying food, but we now know that the type of food we were eating is not very good for you, health-wise.

As you may know, Mexican cuisine is delicious but is often not very nutrient-dense. I absolutely love my culture; it is all about eating, drinking, and having a good time. Tortillas are a staple. We do not only use tortillas for tacos like you might in other parts of the world; we use tortillas in every meal. Eating tortillas is like having water every day in Mexico, and it is a delicious sin.

A multitude of drink options (including beer) are readily available inside every fridge in Mexico. When you visit someone, we tend to offer you a beer instead of water (and it doesn't matter what time it is). Grandma's cooking is always the best, made from scratch, including things like *frijoles de olla* (beans that have been cooked over a low flame for hours), tacos from their leftover meals, and *cafecito con pan* (coffee with sweet pastry). It is a must when you want to catch up with grandma or a friend. We have street tacos available 24 hours a day. When you go out with your friends to a bar, it is a must to stop and get tacos from "Don Panchito," the best in the area. He has the best spicy homemade salsas made from scratch that will help anyone under the influence feel better by the time they get home. There were so many culturally relevant food influences in my life, and because I grew up with them all around me thinking they were "normal," I had no idea that they were not the healthiest options I could reach for. Food and drinks are a very strong paradigm in my country. When you get old enough, you literally drink and eat with your parents, your cousins, your aunts, and your uncles, and you get praised if you drink without getting drunk. It's like a sense of pride we hold for being Mexican; holding our alcohol well is something to brag about.

For the majority of my life, I believed participating in eating and drinking for fun was what I needed to do to fit in with my friends and family so I would not be the boring person in the group. My paradigm was so strong as a Mexican woman, and I believed that it was mandatory to embrace all of these ideas, including overeating and drinking like the majority of my friends and family. I wasn't the healthiest or the fittest Deni during those times. I wasn't willing to change my eating habits because it was like not liking my beautiful genetic makeup; if I dared not participate in drinking beer during events and parties, I feared I would not fit in and would get bullied by everybody.

When I moved to the United States in June of 2010, my life changed completely. I was in an interchange program, living with an American family, and their paradigms were very different from mine. This major cultural transition is among other things that I will expand upon later in this book, but it was one of the major experiences that finally helped me to realize that I was in charge of my health and my body.

You will have your own cultural relationship to food, exercise, celebrations, and what's considered "normal" depending on where you live in the world, how you grew up, and what the people around you were doing and saying about everything in life. This isn't limited to just how you eat and drink, but how you connect with others, communicate, show respect to the people you interact with, manage things in your life, and more. Consider what your own life experience has shown you about how to eat, move, and live in a "healthy" way. What paradigms have you been experiencing in your own life?

We are truly powerful and incredible beings, capable of being the healthiest and happiest humans alive if we decide to do it starting right now. In this book, I will show you how to discover what is holding you back, and show you the steps that will help you reach your health and fitness goals. So open your mind, sit back, relax and keep reading, because this might be the moment your entire life changes. Are you ready?

Part 1:

It's Not You;
It's Your Paradigms

Chapter 1: This Is It

As you know, throughout your life you learn through experiences, cultural habits, opinions, and beliefs. The accumulation of these beliefs and influences becomes what you are right now, in this very moment. All of these elements are called "paradigms," and they basically control the way you perform, dream, walk, interact, reach goals, etc. In order to create real change, you need to study yourself and pay attention to what kind of paradigms are controlling every aspect of your life right now. If you find that it's challenging to reach any type of goal, that you have a hard time moving forward, or that you struggle to take action on things or to truly change your lifestyle habits, the problem isn't you — **it's your paradigms.**

Think about areas in your life that may be holding you back from reaching the goals that you want. This is what this book is all about! We will dig deeper into how to reach your health and fitness goals later, but this book is not about a specific exercise or diet plan. You can eat right and exercise regularly, which will give you short-term results, but if your mind isn't right you will quit at some point or gain back the weight that you lost, and be unhappy with your results overall.

A lot of people start with a goal to attain a healthier version of themselves, but after two or three months, they will quit or make excuses as to why they can't eat healthily. Maybe they think that their life is too busy, that they don't have the resources, or that they aren't ready to give up the convenience of "fast" food and other modern luxuries. I could name hundreds of excuses that might come up in your mind. Most people succumb to these excuses over and over again, creating the same results time after time: I try, I fail, I give up, and I go back to my old patterns. I am going to give you the most powerful way to become the healthiest version of yourself. If you decide to put what I am going to show you in this book into action, you will see long-term results. I can promise you that!

I haven't always been the healthiest version of myself; I grew up in a culture where food and drinks were central components, and this set in place a lot of unwanted paradigms. I never knew what was healthy and what was not; I didn't know about fuelling my body with nutrient-dense foods versus empty-calorie foods. I just knew that I needed to eat in order to live and have energy.

Parents carry their heritage, culture, and paradigms from their ancestors to their children. All the food you like or do not like is literally what your parents and ancestors used to eat or prepare for their loved ones. If you analyze yourself and start digging into your family history, you and your mom may have a favourite meal for breakfast and that meal was the favourite meal of your grandmother or your great-grandpa. Because of this, you get more attached to your eating habits. You may have favourite foods that you eat annually at specific holidays or events, or you may love a specific type of food or method of food preparation solely because that's how your family has "always done things." There is a lot to analyze about the experiences you've had as a child, and how you grow up assuming certain things are "normal" because that's how things have always been. Each of us grew up alongside our family's pre-existing paradigms. I can tell you that, as a Mexican, we take so much pride in our ancestors' recipes and food preparation methods. We pass this knowledge down from generation to generation, and our eating habits aren't what I would call the healthiest. But let me tell you, when I discovered that I held the power in my mind to change this, the beginning of my adventure to freedom began!

Breaking Free from Old Paradigms

I was in high school, and as I mentioned before, my health and eating habits weren't the best. I grew up as a chubby child, and yes, you got it — I was bullied at school and even by my family for my weight. As we know, bullying has a terrible impact on the minds of children, as well as adults. Bullying doesn't have an age restriction. Unfortunately, we all know this still happens through adulthood and doesn't end when we're finished with school. Weight-related bullying can lead to an increase in negative feelings like anxiety, depression, sadness, and more. As a teenage girl, I felt more vulnerable to the negative impact of weight-related bullying due to the importance society places on the body image of women. My mind, my thoughts, and my vulnerability led me to eating disorders. This was the worst war that I've ever confronted inside of my mind. Eating disorders are less about food and more about control. I couldn't control the bullying, mean comments, or interactions with the people who were verbally hurting me — but I could control my food.

Negative thoughts, anger, punishment, and sadness were on my mind constantly. I became so obsessed with my weight and the food that I put into my body. This was the paradigm controlling me at that time. I obsessively tried to control the amount of food that I ate every day, starved myself, and even self-induced vomiting, all in the pursuit of trying to look a certain way.

Sometimes my mother would attempt to force me to eat before bed, and I would stay up late exercising just to burn off those calories. I would not eat at school and starve myself instead. My friends would ask me "aren't you eating today?" I would lie and say that I ate a super big breakfast, or sometimes just eat the lettuce of the sandwich my mom and dad packed me that day.

The reality is that my story is not all that different from MANY women and girls who grow up with the expectation that they should be a certain size and weight in order to be acceptable. Nobody should have to endure ridicule just because they look a certain way, and the standards that are set out by the media and advertising are so difficult to obtain that such a low percentage of women can actually even measure up to those standards naturally. This affects not only the woman who is trying to fit into those standards (often with very unhealthy measures, as I was demonstrating), but also those who are compliant in pushing the idea that only one type of body is good, worthy, and acceptable in the eyes of the media, like the one showcased on all of the swimsuit advertisements and television shows. Those who participate in the bullying are continuing the objectification of women and making the situation worse for young girls who think that their only value is in the number on the scale. This was a big realization for me.

At this time in my life, I danced ballet regularly, so my parents thought that I was losing weight because of all the calories being burned through dance. I had the perfect excuse and thought that I was totally in the clear… until one day, I collapsed!

It was breakfast time and my mom and dad were preparing our meals. Breakfast is a BIG deal in Mexico, and we take our breakfast seriously! My mom asked me to set up the table. I remember my tired and weak body getting up from the couch and reaching for the placemats. After a couple minutes, everything went dark, my hands became cold, and I felt dizzy. I was able to at least yell for my parents because I knew something serious was happening. After that, I don't remember anything.

When I woke up it got worse. I opened my eyes when I was conscious again, but I was blind. I could not see anything but darkness! That was one of the scariest things that has ever happened to me. I started crying and telling my parents that I couldn't see anything. I strongly believe that it was a sign from God because at that moment, I started to pray in my mind and I apologized to my parents and God because I was scared of what I had done to myself. Luckily, after about five minutes or so, my sight came back. My poor parents were so worried. In seeing their faces, and their worry, all I could feel was extreme guilt and shame. That was the moment that made me open my eyes — when I realized that I needed to end this war with myself.

My body and my mind were exhausted from punishing myself by restricting the food I would eat, overexercising, or making myself throw up. It wasn't worth it, and that's all I could think at that moment. I wanted my parents to be happy and my body to feel better. Unfortunately, things like this have to happen to realize that we need to make a change and that we are the only ones responsible for breaking through any challenge in our lives. After this "*no bueno*" (not good) event, I started to realize that I was the one responsible for making a change in my life — no one else would do it for me — but I also needed support from others to stay on track. I am so blessed and grateful that my parents, my family, and my friends helped me through this sour part of my life.

This is one of the events in my life that showed me the power of my mind. Without me working on it regularly, constantly bringing awareness to the internal self-talk that I needed to do, and building my willpower to recover, I'm not sure what would have gotten me through this.

You have the power to create and attract everything you want in your life. False and limiting beliefs, doubts, anxiety, low self-esteem, negative self-image, and negative thoughts are stopping you from getting out there and being the best version of yourself. This is something you can change! If no one has told you this before, though, you may not believe that you are capable of reaching your wildest dreams and fantasies. Yes, you *can* be the healthiest, fittest person you ever dreamed of if you really want to; you *can* build on the natural gifts and talents that God gave you and accomplish whatever it is you dream of. You only live once, and an open mind and knowledge in your life will give you the opportunity to experience abundance, happiness, health — and the ability to achieve any goal that your heart desires.

Open your mind and your heart for new knowledge! Though I cannot be credited for the concepts I will discuss in each chapter and throughout this book, this information is so important and I'm excited to share with you how this has shaped my own life and the lives of many of my clients and friends. I've just studied all of these concepts, and I apply them to my daily life on a consistent basis. Now I'm passing it along to you because I believe if everybody could apply these beautiful treasures into their lives, the world would be a happier and better place.

"

To change what's on the outside, you must change what's on the inside… with faith, love, and persistence!

"

- Tdachi-Deni Whiting

Chapter 2:
Who Do You Think You Are?

"Our self-image, strongly held, essentially determines what we become." -Maxwell Maltz

This quote from Maxwell Maltz is the method that you are going to learn and practice in this first section. This information wasn't discovered by me, but it has been made available to everyone who looks for knowledge and wants a change in their life. As mentioned previously, many of my teachings are from the book *Psycho-Cybernetics*[2] by Dr. Maxwell Maltz, and my coaching program from *Thinking Into Results* by Bob Proctor and Sandy Gallagher. These two powerful sources of information are the main reason that I decided to write this book. These two programs introduced me to the truth that everything in my present experience I created in my past, and that all of it was created in my mind **first**. It made me realize that every single one of us is a powerful walking machine with vibrating energy that can create anything we desire if we use the power of our minds. I want to be very clear that this is not my unique material. The concepts I will be discussing are broad overarching topics and are often ideas that, deep down, we *know* are real and true, but we forget to practice, implement, and embody. Many of the things I will share with you have to do with the repetition of existing, default beliefs. If we hold the same thoughts, doubts, and insecurities and put them on repeat every single day, **we will become what we think** — and our life and results will repeat and never change.

In his book *Psycho-Cybernetics,* Dr. Maltz mentions that if we change our self-image, our personality and our behaviour will

---

[2] Maltz, Maxwell. **Psycho-Cybernetics:** A New Way to Get More Living Out of Life. N. Hollywood, Calif: Wilshire Book, 1976.

change, and in order for this to work, we need consistency. Consistency is a key concept that will create results for us in many areas of our lives. If we want to see results with our external appearance, we need to repeat the behaviours that are congruent to weight changes. If we want to learn a new language, we need to repeat the practice required to retain the new information we're learning. If we want to write a book, we need to show up and write consistently in order to fill a book with words. Remember that there isn't a magic potion. Everything is a process. It didn't take you one day to become who you are, so it won't take one day to change.

The way that you have created your current, existing self-image is through your experiences, and that is literally the secret: *the way that you obtained your current self-image is the same way that you are going to create a new one.* You are going to create new experiences with your beautiful and powerful mind. And it gets better, *amigos* and *amigas*! It has been proven by clinical psychologists that your brain can't differentiate between a real experience and an imaginary one. This is what we are going to learn to do in this chapter.

The person I thought I was when I was younger was a result of experiences in my childhood. During that time, I experienced bullying, low self-esteem, television, friends and others I was exposed to, and the worst toxic thoughts. Everything that I repeated to myself over and over came from the inside. My doubts and insecurities were just voices that I fed into my unconscious, and the voices were regularly telling me that I was fat, ugly, eating too much, and that I needed to punish myself by over-exercising if I ate more than I was "supposed to." The mind is *so* powerful. Most people have no idea how powerful it is, and because of this, that power is used against them. You have unlimited potential, and when you learn how to use your mind to your advantage, the world becomes a very different place. Your mind will dictate who you are and what you attract, *so be careful of what you're thinking about!* Unfortunately, the majority of people will go their entire lives without knowing the power of their thoughts.

The Connection Between Your Mind and Your Health

If, up until this point, you didn't know this either, don't worry! You're in good company. I also did not know that I had the power within me to change everything that was happening in my life. Every single one of us holds a specific "program" in our minds. Even when I had my eating disorder and wasn't overweight anymore, in my mind I still was. I set standards for the image that I wanted to achieve, and that wasn't ideal or healthy for me. I wanted to be and look like other girls in my school, or the celebrities that I saw on television. The exposure to traditional media and the people I held on a pedestal around me set standards for the body types I thought were "acceptable" and "not acceptable." But the reality is that every single body and genetics will always be different. Each body is beautiful in its own way. When it comes to health, everybody will have different goals, and that's okay! Some might want to be fit and have abs, while others want to just move well and have good flexibility. Others still just want to feel good and eat a balanced diet, and they aren't concerned with what size or weight their body is, as long as they know they're eating and moving in a healthy way. It doesn't matter what *your* heart desires, but your main focus should always be on how you nourish and care for your health, and that includes your physical, emotional, and mental health — equally.

There is not just one prototype of the body that is considered healthy, and I think that's where our society has steered us so wrong. Every single one of us is different, and even if you follow a specific diet or a specific routine, your body will never look the same as celebrities, people in magazines, or even someone next to you in the grocery store. You and your best friend could do the exact same fitness program and have exceptionally different results. This is why it is very important you set *health* goals and not focus on losing weight. **You must set health goals that are connected to your feelings.**

Changing or achieving your health goals is definitely a process. If you haven't heard, there are no magic pills or special cleanse drinks that will magically give you results in one day and help you keep them for the rest of your life. Real change takes a dedicated combination of consistency and time, all in the pursuit of a more healthy interior (and potentially exterior!). This is where it helps to shift your mindset to one that is committed to overall health, not just visible results.

Remember, everything in life is a process. Willpower and persistence are a must to achieve *anything* you want in your life. I've been speaking about health and wellness, but this could apply to any area of your life. You need to know that this process is beautiful and exciting if you're willing to look at it this way. You will learn so much about yourself and all the things you can achieve if you just put your mind and your heart into it. I promise you can achieve anything in this world!

At this point, you might be thinking, *"Okay, got it. I'm responsible for my current health. Great. But how in the world do I change it?"* The first and most important step, in my opinion, is to create a brand new image for yourself. A *self-image,* per se. Let's call this new self-image your **"New Power Health Self."** This is the part when you get to study, analyze, and be honest with yourself. Right now you are carrying an image of yourself. That image is the result of everything you are, and what you've accomplished in your life thus far. I'm talking about everything in your beautiful, current being: how you walk, how you talk, how you think, how you take showers, how you raise your kids, how you interact with people, how you eat, and even what you eat. You have adopted all of these methods from your heritage, culture, friends, family, and even your partner. How you do everything in your life, at this very moment, is all based on your existing environment.

The truth is… everything that you have in your life now is no mistake. The way you do things, the people in your life, and your circumstances are all part of what you've been attracting to yourself — what you've been "manifesting" without knowing it. While I do realize that there are many facets to your personal life circumstances (and there are many things that you may consider are not in your control, which is absolutely fair), the way you've been thinking, speaking, and behaving in your life has played a massive role in where you are today. Humans manifest all kinds of things in their lives, and we often manifest things we *don't* want by virtue of continuing to think in the same ways on repeat. So, if you've had a poor self-image for a very long time, no matter what has contributed to making you feel that way, it's no wonder your self-image continues to be negative. If you keep thinking the same things, the same things keep perpetuating. We're going to work on this together.

During this journey, we will be working together and I will be guiding you through every single step and giving you detailed in-structions on what you have to do to have success on your new health journey! Get excited! You will discover the reason why you can't stick to healthy eating habits, why you can't get your butt to move and do any kind of exercise, why you keep eating those sugary snacks and drinks, why you end up quitting before you've reached whatever goal you've set, and, most importantly, you will discover how you can change all of this and become your **"New Power Health Self."** You are going to fall in love with ev-erything you will be learning and putting into practice. Now you will truly understand that being healthy is not just about losing weight, but, more importantly, the beauty of your unique body and the importance of being healthy.

How We're Going to Work Together

As you'll notice throughout your experience with this book, you're going to join information with practice. You're going to put some of the concepts that I'm explaining into action *right away*. One of the best strategies for ensuring that you understand a concept is to implement it with urgency. So, throughout this book, you may see journal pages where you can work through a concept in your own way after it is explained. This way, it isn't just a hypothetical example; it's real and true for you and your circumstances. I encourage you to take the journaling work seriously and complete each exercise entirely. Don't skip pages! The effort you put in will be in direct correlation to the changes you experience — trust me!

JOURNAL EXERCISE 1:

Existing Excuses & Beliefs

To start, I want you to close your eyes and think about beliefs, paradigms, excuses, and experiences that have come up in your life that could be the reason why you haven't reached your health goals. Be very honest with yourself. Maybe you are too harsh on yourself, maybe you don't really think about health and taking care of your body that much, maybe you are in pain and you aren't sure how to execute your goals, or maybe you don't truly believe that the health success you're desiring is possible for you. Think about all of the personal characteristics or traits that you'd describe as a weakness. Think about your current inner self-talk and analyze if it is most often positive talk or negative talk. Do you always give yourself the same excuses? Do you always say yes to something that harms your body for fear of criticism from a group of people you want to fit into? Be honest with yourself. This is a moment for you to take some time to be with no one else but yourself!

Here are some examples of common excuses, beliefs, concerns, and roadblocks to health success:

1. *I don't have the discipline required to reach my health goals.*

2. *I need to look like Jennifer Lopez.*

3. *Having something sweet after a meal is a MUST.*

4. *I am too old to exercise.*

5. *I don't have a workout buddy.*

6. *I get bored easily. Exercise is not fun.*

7. *My finances won't allow me to join a gym or buy healthy food.*

8. *I am too tired. I will start tomorrow.*

9. *I have too much work taking up my time.*

10. *I have too much homework to do.*

11. *My schedule is too busy.*

12. *I am not athletic at all.*

13. *I celebrate with ice cream.*

14. *Life is too short, so I'd better enjoy and eat all I want while I can.*

15. *My schedule doesn't allow me to eat healthy or exercise.*

Do these sound familiar? That's because you're not the only one with these thoughts! Every single human being encounters these thoughts at some point or another, and they unconsciously follow us everywhere we go. Only after recognizing and coming to terms with all of your past excuses and potentially negative beliefs and thoughts are you able to put in the work. The first and most important step is done.

Fill in today's date. This date will mean so much to you when you look back in the future and see how much you have learned about your beautiful being and how much you have accomplished!

Date:

JOURNAL EXERCISE 2:

Evaluating Existing Self-Talk

Next, close your eyes and think about what you tell yourself every day. Have you ever considered this before? Have you ever paid attention to the things you are telling yourself on a regular basis? Consider the below description in order to put into perspective how you might be unconsciously speaking to yourself. These things are commonly referred to as "autosuggestions."[3] Autosuggestion is basically the adoption of ideas, thoughts, and words that you repeat to yourself. These ideas and thoughts will plant themselves into your subconscious mind, which will, by default, change your behaviour and results in life. It is very important that you are truly honest with yourself if you really want to change your health journey. Pay attention to your thoughts, connect with your beautiful being, and start writing everything that comes into your mind. Take as long as you want — dig deep! Review the below timeline and consider where your thoughts would go if you went through an entire day in this way.

You wake up in the morning, open your beautiful eyes, and roll over to the alarm clock ringing quietly beside you. You turn it off and prepare to get out of bed. What is your first thought? Are you excited for the day? Does your body feel good? What might you tell yourself about your body as you get out of bed and walk toward the bathroom? You enter the bathroom and jump in the shower. You glance at your body in the mirror. What is your first thought? How do you assess your body in the mirror? What do you think as you escape your own reflection and get into the shower? Are you happy to see yourself in the mirror? Do you think something positive and loving, or negative and damaging? After your shower, you get dressed and head downstairs to prepare breakfast. How does your meal experience feel? Do you look in

---

[3] https://www.dictionary.com/browse/autosuggestion?s=t

the fridge and get excited about what you're about to make? Do you complain that there isn't anything "healthy" in there and that you "can't" eat something nourishing for your body? Do you pull out your breakfast ingredients with excitement and joy, or fear and loathing? Are you looking forward to fuelling your body? What might you tell yourself subconsciously about your cooking knowledge, skill, or ability? You finish breakfast and are now thinking about how you should probably exercise after work today. Are you excited to complete physical activity after work? Or do you tell yourself you'll probably be too tired to do that after you've finished work? What might you be telling yourself about your ability or availability to complete your workout? Are you too busy? Will it wait until tomorrow? You get home after work and it was a long day. Do you grab a drink to loosen up to? Do you grab the quickest thing to eat and just sit back on the couch? Or maybe you say you have no time to move your body, but then you realize it is almost midnight and you spent two hours scrolling on social media?

This is an example of how you might continue to consider your daily lifestyle and what thoughts may be permeating your subconscious. The thing is, we all think thousands of thoughts per day, and many of them are not ones that we analyze logically, pay attention to, or file away with an accurate label. It takes a very high degree of emotional and self-awareness to notice a thought and categorize it as negative or unhelpful. You may look at yourself in the mirror every morning and think something like: *Ugh. I really need to lose weight.* In your head, this thought is so short-lived, brief, tiny, and seemingly insignificant that you dismiss it as "nothing" and move on with your day. Maybe you've never paid attention to the thoughts passing your mind when you do or experience certain things. **Now is the time to start paying attention.** Even seemingly small thoughts like that — occurring regularly *over time, with consistency* — will generate "results," but this time they are creating negative results, keeping you in exactly the same place that you are in **right now.** Are you making sense of this now? It makes sense that, to lose weight, *we must act and behave in a way with consistency over time* that will generate the results we desire. So why wouldn't it make sense that the negative beliefs and self-talk that you've never paid attention to — the things that you repeat in your head over and over — **have played a huge role in where you are exactly in your life at this moment?**

Your turn! What goes through your head on a daily basis? Use the space below to write your own version. Be honest and open about what really goes on in your head!

Date:

Creating a New Power Health Self

In this section, you will be using the excuses that you already identified for yourself in Journal Exercise 1 — the *"no bueno"* habits you have already, that you now know as your existing paradigms — to write new ones. Now you have all of the thoughts, beliefs, and damaging ideas that affect your subconscious mind. These paradigms are the ones that won't allow you to reach the health and fitness goals that you want. Isn't it funny that every single one of us *knows* what is holding us back? We do know — whether we've been paying attention or not — but the interesting part is that we do not make a change. If we know exactly what is holding us back from reaching our health goals, then why don't we make the necessary changes to get where we want to be?

This is because the way we live our lives is like our programming. The habits that we repeat every single day are often unconscious, and we don't take the time to observe what we're doing; we just *do.* Unless we do something about it, our lives will absolutely not change. These habits will stay with us for the rest of our lives (and not only as it relates to our health goals). Every single paradigm and habit will affect our lives in various different ways and will affect our results overall. Consider this: if you don't already have everything the way you want it to be in your life, how do you expect to get the things you want while walking the same old path that you've always walked? It is very important to take this content and work seriously if you really want to change your health.

You might be thinking, *how in the world will this work and help me?* I know it sounds crazy, and like a fiction book. It isn't. *It is true,* I promise! I didn't create or invent these concepts, but I have seen them work for me. With this information, lots of people are joining me in taking responsibility for themselves so that they can truly change their lives. You can do this, too!

But First, What *is* Health?

Now that you have identified what is holding you back, we will work together on creating a shift in your mind. In order to do this, we will be creating your new health image. Remember when I mentioned that your mind can't differentiate between a real experience and an imaginary experience? We will be using both real experiences and imaginary experiences along with repeated affirmations (positive statements) to ingrain the new thoughts and patterns into your conscious and subconscious mind. Real experiences are very important in your health journey. Your mind will help you accomplish these until you get to a point where you do not want to go back to that old, unhealthy, unmotivated self-image that you had. Real experiences will give you confidence and keep you motivated. This is why it is so important that you work with the imaginary ones — so that you can act on real experiences.

Before you start creating your new healthy self-image, let's review a couple of things. I want to give you some insights into what it means to be healthy. It is very important to analyze this, because maybe your thoughts about being healthy aren't exactly ideal. The view of health is not necessarily only being super "fit," having excellent nutrition habits, and always being mindful of your weight. Health involves so much more than those things. If you research health in any capacity, you're likely to find varying definitions, health experts, dietitians, and even doctors that will tell you that a specific diet is the one that you need to follow. If you ask me what my favourite definition is, I would say, "Health is a state of complete physical, mental, and social well-being, and not merely the absence of disease or infirmity."

But what you need to focus on when creating your new **Power Health Self** is not what actresses or actors look like, a specific diet your coworker likes, or that influencer on the internet who tells you what to drink or eat. What you really need to focus on is how your beautiful self wants to feel in terms of overall health. Why? Because being healthy can mean different things to different people. It's subjective.

So, I am going to give you some tips before you start focusing and writing down your new self-image. This part is super important because it will allow your definition of health to be more attached to you. You are going to feel inspired to reach your goal, and your feelings will be more involved in the process. This is what will help you go and not quit. Review the three points below to help you create a smarter perception of health and to get you on the right track.

JOURNAL EXERCISE 3:

Power Health Self Prep Work

*1. Think about how you want to feel physically, mentally, and emotionally. Use your mind and imagine how you will act and feel when you become that healthier person. For example, I want my new **Power Health Self** to be less stressed, less tired, have a better mood, feel energized, crave better foods, or not get sick as often.*

---

2. Use the list you created before regarding your paradigms and damaging ideas about your current self-image for health that will help you get an idea of what you want to reinforce for this coming journey.

---

3. Do not worry now about what you need or how you are going to achieve this new healthy image. ONLY focus on how you want to feel physically, mentally, and emotionally. Write down how you want to feel in those ways here.

Now, using these tips, you need to get to work. Review the excuses, paradigms, doubts, and beliefs that you wrote down in Journal Exercise 1. After reading them, you are going to put your mind to work. Play some calming music, sit back, and relax.

Close your eyes and think about how your new **Power Health Self** wants to feel — maybe more motivated, less stressed, more confident, happier, etc. How do you want to look? Maybe you want to fit in those jeans that you used to wear before your pregnancy. Maybe you have a trip coming up and want to wear that beautiful swimming suit that you saw in the store. Whatever comes to your mind, be super clear and super detailed. This is one of the most powerful tools we are going to use to create your new self-image. Write it all down. Have fun and take as long as you want. You need to feel it and get excited, because this is what will keep you going until you reach your new **Power Health Self**.

Are you ready? GO!

Think, Imagine and Then...Take *Action*

Here it comes...the most exciting part! Now that you have created the list of how you *want* to feel as a new, healthy human being, we're going to be creating tools that will help you create experiences that are aligned with your new vision. Remember when I told you earlier that your brain can't differentiate between a real experience and an imaginary experience? Well, we will be working with both in this chapter.

Imaginary experiences are extremely powerful. As Dr. Maxwell Maltz says in his book: *If we can imagine our desires with details and emotions as if they were already accomplished, our brains will accept it as a real experience.*[4] These imaginary experiences will help you support your real experiences. The real experiences will impact your life dramatically, and when you reach the new healthy self that you want, your mind and body won't want to go back to that old, unhealthy self-image.

I mentioned earlier that I lived in Mexico almost all of my life. At that point, I had a self-image, but the truth is that we have different self-images throughout our lives. Moving to the United States was one step closer to a healthier self-image for me. I was in an exchange program and I lived with a wonderful American host family (Hello Heather and Richard, if you are reading my book!). I was taking care of their kids and studying English. Everything was new for me. I was experiencing a brand new language and culture. Their lifestyle and health habits were different from mine. I was in a new house, and I did not have my family and friends nearby. I didn't have my friends to go out with, and I didn't have the same routine. I did not have my mother telling me to eat more or having the tacos of "Don Panchito" waiting for me around the corner on a Friday night. I experienced a completely new life that helped me realize that there were better choices out there. I was now in charge of my choices. I met and built new

[4] Maltz, Maxwell. Psycho-Cybernetics: A New Way to Get More Living Out of Life. N. Hollywood, Calif: Wilshire Book, 1976.

friendships with people from all over the world that helped me with my new self-image, and little by little I achieved who I wanted to be.

You are going to be creating these experiences with your mind, and in reality. These experiences will become *you*. Your mind and body will be wherever you want them to be, but it is important to mention that this is a process — and on this journey, you will need to put in some work. Real change does not happen overnight. It's important for you to find joy in the journey, otherwise you'll be disappointed with the destination.

It is imperative that you have a clear and very strong purpose for doing this work; your "why" helps to ignite your willpower, persistence, and belief in yourself. The exciting part is: that's it! This isn't some crazy, complicated system! It is free and it only depends on you! Only you can achieve it. No one else will do it for you — not your parents, your friends, your partner, your kids, or your colleagues. They can be a support system for you, but the real work begins and ends with you. The good news is that you can totally do this, and we will do it together. I will give you the tools, and you will commit yourself to doing whatever it takes to be the healthy person you always wanted to be.

New Habits Take Time

You now know that it takes at least 21 days to create a habit, which is essentially the time it takes for our mind to reprogram themselves. You need not judge yourself or your results during this journey. I can't tell you this enough. This is a step-by-step, slow, progressive journey. Just like a physical journey, you need to prepare yourself for a big change. In the same way that you wouldn't want to physically run a marathon before preparing yourself mentally and physically, you don't want to tackle all of this mindset work without preparing first.

Commit to at least 21 days of consistent and persistent work. Tell your old self-image *baby, bye, bye, bye!*[5] When your old, annoying self–image tries to pull you back and tell you things like *you can't do it, you are wasting your time, you're never going to change…* you need to stop, breathe, and show those old squeaky paradigms, damaging ideas, doubts, and insecurities that you are different now, and you won't give up. Your self-image should be growing throughout your life. Without growth, you will feel lost, unmotivated, and without a purpose, but sometimes our old selves feel fear and discomfort at the prospect of making a change — so they resist. This is normal.

Now that you have your list of all of your new habits and updated desires that make up your new Power Health Self, you need to write them out like you already are that healthy person you want to be. Yes, that's right. You are going to write them out *as if they already exist. Present tense.* I did not invent this technique,[6] but it is powerful. Remember, don't judge the strategies; instead, consider that this basic technique has helped many, many other people get the results they desired. This is proven work.

I am going to give you an example of how your new **Power Health Self** "script" will look. You can use some of these examples, but try not to just copy them; rather, adjust them for yourself and your own personal circumstances. You are the only YOU in the world. There is no other you, so your script has to be created for and belong to **you only.**

5 N'sync fans? Anyone?
6 This was learned inside Proctor-Gallagher's Thinking Into Results program. https://www.proctorgallagherinstitute.com/

Example of *Power Health Self* Statements:

I am so happy and proud of myself for the healthy person I have become.

I am so happy and grateful that all of the cells and organs in my body work perfectly fine.

I am so energized because I feed my body with healthy food and God gives me power over food.

I always stop eating when I am full and satisfied, and I celebrate in ways that support my health.

My body is strong, and I love when my heart works hard. I do not stop when I am tired; I stop when I am done. I love working out and the energy that it gives me after I am done.

I am stronger than any excuse, and I am grateful that I have the chance to improve every day.

I am worthy of a body I love, and I love my body for everything amazing it can do.

JOURNAL EXERCISE 4:

Power Health Self Script

This is just an example of a healthy script you can use. Take your time and add as much as you want to your **Power Health Self** script. Do not rush. Really study and be clear on what being healthy means to you, and not to others. Always remember that you are doing this for yourself. You are really writing down how you want to feel, the goals you want to achieve, and how this new self-image will help you live the rest of your life. If you need to change anything in your script, you can go back and do it. Make sure this script makes your soul happy, excited, and empowered, and that you can't wait to work on that new healthy person you want to be.

My New Power Health Self Script

Taking Inspired Action

The action part is coming, and I believe you are going to love it. Now that you have a clear vision of where you want to go and who you want to become, we will get the job done together. Your mind learns through experiences and repetition, and we are going to create both of them now. This is where you need to put on your imaginary cape and become your own superhero to make this happen. Now you know all the insecurities, doubts, bad habits, and paradigms that stop you from getting the results you want. It's time to execute.

Mis amigos y amigas, if you are reading this book, you have the power — and that power is within you. It is free. It is available to you 24 hours a day. You do not need anybody else to walk down this path. You do not need to drive far away, spend thousands of dollars, or learn some very complex system in order to gain access to a better version of yourself. Today is the day when all of the power inside of you is going to come out. You are totally ready for this, and I absolutely believe in you.

How To Incorporate This Work Daily

You will be working with three exercises that are going to reset that self-image that you do not want, but remember, it takes at least 21 days for your brain to adjust to your new habits and what you command it to think and do. Persistence and consistency are key. With persistence, everything is possible. Quitting is not an option, because we are talking about your health. You need to do this if you want to feel and look and live better. You are worthy of a body you love, and that amazing well-being feeling that comes with it.

The script that you just created will be your best friend for a while. You are going to use it until you reach your ideal Power Health Self. This script might change or improve in the future, but your script will become your new **you**.

The first step is repetition. You will read, write, and listen to your script every day. The secret here is not to read it over and over until you are sick of it, pulling your hair out, and asking your-self *what on Earth is the point of all this!?* Instead, you need to use your beautiful imagination and feelings to trust and have faith that this is the way to become the healthy person you want to be. There is no perfect way to do this. You have done this before. Think of something in your life that transpired after you thought about it constantly for a long time.

This is how it works: Throughout your life, everything you *currently* have is because of your beliefs, your paradigms, and your current self-image. At some point in your life, you were thinking of who you are and what you have become. Now is the time to think, imagine, and create your new you. This is how we are going to do it:

> **Número Uno:** You will use your script every day — when you wake up, before bed, when you are at lunch — you can do it as many times as you want. The more you do it, the better you are going to get at it. This is how we are going to create the imaginary experiences in your mind, and your brain won't have any idea that they are not true! (Sorry brain, we will trick you.)

This step is called visualization, and you have done it all your life without knowing it — like when you met your husband and you thought "this is it, he's the One." You imagined yourself walking down the aisle with him, and pictured the type and style of dress you wanted to wear. Or what about when you picture the car you are driving currently? Didn't you fantasize about seeing yourself driving it and picking up your friends to go for a ride? Crazy, right? You will do the exact same thing now, but with your health. Here is where you will imagine, feel, and put all of your faith. You will imagine and see yourself as if it is happening right now: how happy and healthy you are; eating those healthy, yummy meals. You will see and imagine yourself going to the gym because now you are motivated and energized. You will feel chills and feel so much excitement.

It's like being a kid again, fantasizing without knowing how you'll do it, and no one stopping you from following your dreams. Use as many senses as you can. What does it look like? Are there any smells, tastes, or feelings you can picture? The more you do it — and the more you do it with detail — the more real it is going to feel.

> **Número Dos:** Record yourself reading your self-image script, or, even better, write it throughout the day in your journal. Writing it down will help to ingrain it into your brain, but remember that when you do this exercise, you need to **feel it**. You can repeat this 100 times a day, but without using emotion or faith, you won't be able to trick your brain. I'll give a clear example. Imagine a couple saying to each other, "I love you." When that person is feeling it and using emotion, it will transmit that feeling to the other person, and that person will feel it and believe it. But now imagine when a person just says "I love you" with the sentiment of a cold fish, zero energy or emotion… the other person wouldn't feel anything, and wouldn't believe that person has any feelings toward her. That is the key; you can't be doing your visualizations with lacklustre energy. You need to do this with gumption and enthusiasm.

If you don't set your mind to believing that you can consume better foods, then you will never put a healthy meal into your mouth. If you do not set your mind to knowing that you are capable of doing more movement with your body — more walks, or signing up for the *gym — then you will never make time for it. This is it; you control it and have the superpowers to achieve it. Use your imagination and your mind to bring your Super **Power Health Self** into reality.*

> ***Número Tres:*** Each day, with every little thing that you do during the day that brings you into a real-life experience mirroring what you've been visualizing, please do me a favour and c*elebrate* it! It does not matter how little or big it is. You need to stop and congratulate yourself, by speaking it out loud: *"Great job Deni! You didn't drink that soda at lunch today, you ordered water! You are a beast!"* Or, *"Great job, Deni. You parked your car in the farthest parking spot to get more steps in. Way to go!"* You need to get in the habit of celebrating the small things. Write them down in your journal or just speak them out loud, but make sure you take note and become aware of the small successes you're having.

These are three basic exercises that are super easy and won't take you long. They will reprogram your mind and motivate you to reach the goal you want. Remember, your current self-image will want to fight you, pull you down, and send doubts to your brain, but you have to fight. This is completely normal. You are not alone. This is the entire process. It's simple. With these exercises, you *will* start reprogramming your mind — as long as you take it seriously and practice consistently.

If you feel discouraged one day, read this chapter as many times as you want. It will help you as a reminder that everything you are doing is a process, and it is completely on you to keep moving forward. You will be working with your new self-image script every day. Keep up the good work, I absolutely believe in you!

In the next chapter, we are going to be talking about your health and fitness goals. Now that you have a clear picture of your perfect Power Health Self, it will be easier to set clear goals. The script that you created in this chapter will help you and hold your hand while achieving the goals you set. With these three exercises, you will be working with your mind to create those imaginary experiences. We are now going to be creating real-life experiences with the goals that we set in the coming chapter.

"

Setting goals is the first step in turning the invisible into the visible.

"

- Tony Robbins

Chapter 3:
Your "Why" and Your Goals

I love this quote from Tony Robbins: *"Setting goals is the first step in turning the invisible into the visible."* He is absolutely right. If you want to achieve anything in your life, you need to have goals. Milestones and achievements that you desire will then become your reality. These goals will help you measure your progress. You need to at least know the end goal that you'd like to achieve and have a clear picture of it, because without a clear image of where you want to go, you won't know the steps that you have to take in order to reach your goals — in life or in health. Creating and setting goals is so important because the process will hold you accountable and encourage you to keep going.

The self-image script that you created as a foundational step in Chapter 1 will now help you to create your goals in this chapter. Before we get to that, we will be working on your "why." You will never stick to a plan and get to your goals if you don't know *why* you want to do it. You need to find and understand what is driving you to achieve the changes you want to see. You need to really think about your "why."

The past journaling exercises helped you to get an idea of what limiting beliefs are holding you back, what health means to you, and the kinds of things that you want to embody in your vision (your **Power Health Self** script). But now I want you to think about *why* you want to feel and look that way. Why is this important to you?

You must have a very strong emotional connection to the reason for your change, as this will help you achieve your fitness goals.

Just like our goals and life vary from person to person, you and I will have very different *reasons* for working toward our goals and executing on our intended vision. The reason I decided to change my health when I had my eating disorders and fainted that day was because I wanted to feel better, have more energy, and I did not want my parents to suffer and be worried about me. And, of course, I didn't want to feel like I was at war with myself on a daily basis, battling bad thoughts in my mind 24 hours a day. These strong, emotionally attached reasons made me come up with a strong, emotional "why" that preceded any changes I made.

You may have seen or heard stories about relationships falling apart, and then one partner makes a complete lifestyle change and completely redefines their appearance after the break-up. Or perhaps you've heard of someone who has received bad news from their doctor, who tells them that they have to lose weight because their life is at risk. These exemplify what it means to have a very powerful "why"; it could almost be defined as a source of motivation behind your drive to change, and it helps keep you moving forward even when things get hard. However, it isn't necessary to go through a break-up or get doctor-delivered bad news in order to have a spark of motivation. You just need to understand your deep-rooted "WHY."

You can simply be driven by the fact that you want to feel better, be able to keep up with your kids, play with your grandkids, be pain-free, or live a longer and healthier life. Your reasons don't have to be life or death, with an all-or-nothing energy. You just need something to come back to when you're struggling. I am going to give you some tips that will help you come up with a clear and strong "why." Remember: you need to use your emotions and your emotional connections to bolster your reasons, so you clearly understand why you want to achieve your goals. You need to *feel* it because you will be more driven, and every time you want to give up you will have this "why" to bring your motivation back up.

I want you to read your **Power Health Self** script again; that will really take you to the place where you want to be. Imagine that all of those goals you are going to set in this chapter are already achieved, but now that you have achieved these goals in your script, I want you to imagine and think about what you are going to be doing and feeling with that new self-image.

These questions will help you write down a clear "why." Ask yourself the following questions, and write down your answers on the journal pages provided:

Why is eating healthily important to me?
Why is fitness important to me?
Why is being healthy important to me?
Who will be with you when you become that person?
What are you going to be able to do?
How are you feeling when you become that person?

Use these questions to guide you and write down your "why" in the space below. Make sure your "why" is full of meaning and emotion.

JOURNAL EXERCISE 5:

Uncovering Your Why

I want you to think about this. We all know of some crazy success stories of different people around the world. They were either in a very tough situation and they needed to make a change because their life was at risk, or they simply wanted to prove to themselves or somebody else that they could do the thing that they wanted to do. They used that reason as a *burning desire* to do whatever it took to get there. **You need to find that desire inside of you — a "why" that will keep you going no matter what.**

Here is an example of a *"no muy bueno"*[7] (not very good) "why": *I want to be healthy because I want to feel energized and happy.*

This is a **no muy bueno** "why," because, although it has a valid reason (you want to feel energized and happy), it doesn't elicit any personal emotion.

Here is a better example. This is a **bueno**[8] (good) "why":

I want to be healthy and fit because I want to be able to keep up with my kids. I want to play and do activities with them and not feel exhausted afterwards. I want to be a good role model for my family. I want to live a healthy and long life so that my kids can have a mommy/daddy in their lives — and so that we can make memories together — for as long as possible.

I want you to come up with a "why" like this. One that sets your heart on fire. One that goes deeper than just surface level. Work on your "why" before we continue with your goals. It is very important. You can set up any goal you want, but if you do not have a strong meaningful reason, it will be very hard to keep up with this journey. Have fun, write it down, and anchor in the reason behind your desired change. You've got this!

---

[7]No muy bueno: C'mon, you can do better than that. Not good!
[8]Bueno: Good!!! You've got this now. Are you feeling it?

JOURNAL EXERCISE 6:

Your "Why"

Creating Smart Goals is Key

If you are reading this, it means that you have written your "why," and this "why" will help you throughout your journey. Now, we are going to talk about goals. Having good, solid goals will give you power toward your success — but creating goals can often be easier said than done. You have to set smart goals, and they shouldn't be driven by underlying fears or body image issues.

When I had eating disorder issues in my teenage years, my mind was full of insecurities. I wanted to look like this professional athlete or the girls on the TV. I set up unattainable goals based on my paradigm at that time. I had no idea what would take me there. I just wanted to look like that, and that took me to unhealthy and harmful options. Remember to set your goals about how you want to feel and what will make you happy, not how other people look and how you measure up. If the goals you are setting are rigid, they will bring you anxiety. If they don't feel right or they are unrealistic, you will most likely quit in a short period of time.

When I started my journey, I started with one or two goals at a time. When you start achieving those little goals, your mind and body will start engaging. Quick wins are satisfying and set you on the path to working on something even bigger. While you cannot physically lose 20 pounds overnight and accomplish your goal with that kind of speed, you can celebrate cutting down on your late-night snack habit, or getting in the right amount of water in a day. Those little things are in your control and are worth honouring and celebrating, as mentioned in Chapter 1.

After these real-life experiences of achieving some of your initial goals, you absolutely can start to set your sights on bigger goals. A lot of people want to eat healthily, cut sugar, go to the gym, and meal prep all at once. Trying to do that much at once will make you feel overwhelmed and more likely to give up because it's too difficult to do everything at once in the beginning. What's worse is if (in your mind) you fail at one little thing that you were trying to accomplish, you will start attracting negativity into your mind, and you will go back to that old self-image you do not want to perpetuate. Instead, I will be guiding you so that you can set smart goals that will bring you to those real-life experiences with which we want to reprogram your mind.

I want you to go back to Journal Exercise 1 & 2 (pages 37-41 & 42-45) where you wrote down all of your excuses and insecurities in the self-image chapter. These paradigms will help you set your goals. You have already identified all of your weaknesses, and we will start by tackling one at a time at the beginning of this journey. When you are aware of what is pulling you down, it will make it so much easier for you to facilitate change around that habit. These goals will be your "short-term goals," and this will build your confidence and competence in a shorter period of time. This, my friends, is the real experience we want to create. Remember: you need both *real* and *imaginary* experiences to start tricking and reprogramming your mind.

Your long-term goal will be the exercise we did in Chapter 2 as well Journal Exercise 3 (pages 43-45). *What does being healthy mean to you?* Remember, I gave you my favourite definition of health at the beginning of the book: *"Health is a state of complete physical, mental, and social well-being and not merely the absence of disease or infirmity."* You do not have to adopt the same exact definition of health as me, but I would encourage you to consider that health is not many of the things that you likely thought it was based on what we're often taught growing up.

Contrary to what magazines, advertising, and the film and television industries have taught us, health is not only being skinny. Health constitutes so much more than that. It is impossible to tell the health of a person from just looking at them from the outside, and there are plenty of people who are exceptionally unhealthy and yet have a small frame. It is just not a fair indication of health, and you deserve to break free from this old notion that slim = healthy. Consider this as you start contemplating your personal health goals.

Setting Short-Term Goals for Quick Wins

This will be one of the most exciting parts of your journey. You are going to go back and review your excuses from your old self-image, and you will convert them into short-term goals. These small goals will allow you to gain confidence and create real experiences that will help your mind feel more confident. These small goals will lead you to bigger goals.

Take a look back at your journal from page 39 and you will be able to analyze all of the things that are currently holding you back. We will be tackling every single one of these habits and excuses one at a time. Remember, the goal here is not to feel overwhelmed. We want to gain confidence little by little to achieve our bigger goals.

You are going to sort that list and ask yourself, "Which of these excuses, bad habits, or doubts are holding me back most from becoming my **Power Health Self?**" Pick one or two from that list, and remember that you can always add more any time you want. We will be working with these lists for three weeks at a time. After these three weeks, we will add one or two more.

The way we're analyzing and setting short-term goals will allow us to have more controllable outcomes that will affect our long-term goals, but aren't things that are out of our control. They allow us to manage the direction we want to go, even if we don't have a destination on the GPS yet. You can't control if and when you lose a certain amount of weight and on what timeline, but if you make a decision to cut out alcohol for 30 days, or drink a gallon of water per day, you know that you can control those things, and the results are not ambiguous. You either drink the gallon of water per day, and accomplish the thing you set out to do, or you don't. You either avoid alcohol for 30 days, or you don't. They are easier to manage, track, and complete because it is possible to complete them in a 24 hour period — unlike weight loss, strength gain, or dropping a clothing size. We start here because you have the power to control your destiny, so to speak, and that power will become contagious and like fuel for you to continue rising toward your long-term goal.

For example, you may think, "I do not know what to prepare or how to cook healthy recipes… My coworkers bring pastries every morning and I can't say no… I need my soda to pick my energy back up in the middle of the day…" Or, maybe you are a parent and you use your kids as an excuse for not having time when there are so many things you can do with them to move and have fun.

I really need you to be honest with yourself, because this is your mind and your body, and what you tell yourself is how your mind and body will react.

Look at that list on the page that I mentioned before (page 39). Write down a list of short-term goals. For example, if one of your paradigms or excuses was: "I need my soda to pick my energy back up in the middle of the day," one of your short-term goals could be to *cut down soda intake by one can per day.* If your paradigm is: "I love my coffee with two tablespoons of sugar, otherwise it doesn't taste good," your short-term goal could be: *I will use only one tablespoon of sugar,* or, *I will use a natural sweetener that is better for my body.* These short-term goals are my favourite. They will give you a feeling of immediate accomplishment when you achieve them. It does not matter how small and silly you think they are. Remember, every little step will take you to your final goal: your new **Power Health Self.**

Short Term Goals

Setting Your First Long-Term Goal

Your long-term goal is very important. Often, when you set these goals, you focus on the wrong ideas — like dropping a specific number of pounds, fitting into your old clothes, or trying to look like a specific celebrity. These are not healthy goals to set because there are so many variables influencing whether you are capable of achieving them or not. That's not to say you can't have a weight loss goal if that's something that's important to you, but if you're so fixated on the EXACT number you are hoping to lose, and then you don't hit it quickly or you don't hit it *exactly*, chances are you're going to perpetuate that disappointed feeling that we discussed earlier. Imagine if you were dead set on losing 25 pounds, and after six months of focus, you had only lost 15? Does the exact number matter if you know you did other incredible things like successfully changing your habits, cutting back on things like drinking alcohol, eating sugar, or eating processed foods? You created a new fitness habit and noticed your clothes fitting better, but you are so fixated on the number 25 that you feel unsuccessful. That's not a way to live your life!

Your long-term goal will become easier to achieve when you start tackling and checking off your short-term goals. Remember that you cannot run without crawling, walking, and training first. It's important that you set both short and long-term goals to stay on track.

You now know your "why," and you know some of the smaller, short-term goals that you are planning to begin to tackle. **What long-term goal do you want to achieve?** Sit and think about this for a while before you write it down in the space provided. Use the below questions to prompt you, if you're having trouble:

What is important to you in your health?
What would hitting this goal mean to you?

How long do you think it will take to accomplish your long-term goal?

What are you going to do on the days that it seems hard to achieve this goal?

How are you going to celebrate on the way toward your goal, and when you reach it?

Long Term Goal

It is important that you keep a close eye on this goal that you've written down. I suggest you write it on a Post-It note and put it somewhere you'll see it every day, like the bathroom mirror, the fridge, or even at your workplace. Alternatively, you could take a photo of what you wrote down with your phone, and then set that photo as your lock screen so that you see it every time you look at your device. (That way you're guaranteed to see it about five hundred times per day, right? Ha!)

It's Easy To Keep Your Word to Others; It's Easier To Break Your Word to Yourself

You completed the easiest part; when you are excited about something or you start a new journey, your energy and focus are at such a high level that you're ready to go, and you don't think anything will ever get in your way. But for some reason, you can often let go of the goal and do not finish what you start. This is a pattern you have experienced before, I'm sure. You know… you slack off, you start eating fast food, and your discipline is not the same as it was in the beginning. Life, kids, and social events come your way and interrupt your momentum. The crazy part is that you know it, and you just make excuses. It's easier to make excuses than to keep accountability to yourself. We're going to break that cycle.

The best part is that YOU and only YOU can get your butt back on track. NO ONE ELSE IS GOING TO BE BEHIND YOU, and NO ONE ELSE IS RESPONSIBLE FOR YOUR SUCCESS. It's no one's job to make sure that you go to your workout classes, wake up earlier so you have more free time during the day, or plan your meals on the weekend. It's up to YOU to execute these things.

I know making changes can be hard, but I am going to give you some tips that will help you get back on track when you feel like you are coming back to your old *"no bueno"* unhealthy self.

1. *Use your journal, or create a health calendar. Plan your days and your meals. Do not aim to be perfect. Little steps each day count.*

2. *Recognize time wasters. Yes, we all have them, and we are human. Maybe you spend too much time on the phone, in front of the TV, or maybe you just wake up late. You need to be honest and schedule your times for exercise and movement.*

3. *Read and repeat your big goal and mini-goals daily. Keep them in a place where you can see them, listen to your recording, or write them down whenever you have a chance.*

4. *Embrace discomfort. This is one of the things I tell my clients over and over. It is not easy to get out of your comfort zone, but if you never just do it and suck it up, you will never grow. Every single human being goes through this — you are not the only one. Remember that.*

5. *Get an accountability partner. It can be anyone who you trust and who understands your desire to create change in your life. People crave and require support systems for many changes they experience in life. We need someone to push us through sometimes, and vice versa.*

6. *Make your goals public. You can use social media and announce it to the world, or you can tell your partner, mom, cousin, or coworker. This will put some pressure on you, and you will be more focused on making it happen if you catch yourself slacking or making excuses.*

7. *Make it happen. Take action every day, and every time you catch yourself slacking or making excuses, change your attitude and go back to your goal. It's okay — just press the RESET button and start again tomorrow.*

It is important that you are aware that life is going to happen, and that you do not need to be perfect. If you're only able to execute on your healthy habits when you're alone, in your house, with full control over the food, you're going to miss out on a lot of life! The only thing you need to remember is that you are working toward your healthiest self, and it doesn't matter what happens. You need to keep working toward that goal little by little, with a positive attitude. Pause and think about how hard your body works every day, the constant work you do while you sleep, eat, or work. Your heart and your other organs are always there for you, and you need to remember to nourish your body with good food and movement.

Take some time to appreciate what your body does for you, and consider how you treat it even when it does all of these things for you by default. Then, think even deeper about how you think and how you speak about your body. Are the things that you think and say *kind*, or *hurtful?* In the next chapter, you will learn how important self-talk is. Maybe you haven't noticed it, but every single day you are telling yourself words that make you act a certain way. Self-talk is important not only for your health but also for daily life. Self-talk is the gateway of behavioural change, so you'd better be telling the right things to yourself.

Talk to yourself with kindness and positivity; you are your own biggest cheerleader.

- Tdachi-Deni Whiting

Chapter 4:
The Internal Dialogue

Every day you have internal conversations with yourself, and most of the time you do not notice what the heck you are telling yourself! This comes back to your self-image. Your self-talk reveals your thoughts, beliefs, questions, and ideas. Self-talk can be negative or positive. It can be encouraging or mean-spirited, friendly or stressful. The reason self-talk is so important to discuss is because you are in charge of it. You have the power to change what is not working for you toward your life or your health. It doesn't matter what is going on outside. It doesn't matter what people tell you. You are your best cheerleader, and only YOU know what dialogue is circulating around your headspace.

Self-talk will enhance your health, the way you perform in your workouts, and how you perform in life. You just have to be aware of what you tell yourself so that you can learn how to use it in an effective, helpful way. It has the potential to assist you with your eating habits, action habits, and how you push yourself during your workouts.

When I was young, my inner dialogue was a vicious circle. This is not uncommon for adolescents, and while I can only speak about my experience as a girl, teenager, young adult, and woman, I know that negative inner dialogue is not something that discriminates based on gender or sexual orientation. Everyone has internal dialogue, and everyone has experienced critical self-talk at one point or another. As a young girl, my internal dialogue was completely negative, and I punished myself with words that made me take **"no bueno"** actions. These *"no bueno"* actions hurt my health, confidence, and personality. The worst part is that no one did this to me; I did it to myself.

Now I look back and know how important it is that we're mindful of the things we say to ourselves, silently or verbally. I know the benefits of becoming a more optimistic-minded person, not one who is pessimistic by default. I know how important it is to become an encourager and a positive thinker — someone who sees the world's glass as half-full — not someone who is a "Debbie Downer." In a study published in the Proceedings of the National Academy of Sciences,[9] research showed that optimistic people have a better quality of life, health, and longevity. So, if I haven't convinced you yet, you need to learn and practice positive self-talk for your own health! This positive talk will enhance your performance and general well-being. I promise!

You might be wondering, *how do I start shifting my behaviour and, thus, my life?* First of all, you need to be aware of what you tell yourself, and identify all the negative things you play on repeat inside your head. Remember when we discussed consistency in Chapter 2? Consistency can work in non-beneficial ways, too. If you're regularly playing a soundtrack of negativity inside your head, even when nobody else has a clue what you're thinking about, how do you think that affects your mood, energy, and vibration level? We are going to go deeper into positive and negative self-talk, and I am going to help you identify the negative parts so that you can get rid of them. Before we begin, I want you to know this: The more you work on improving the quality and positivity level of your self-talk, the easier you'll find it to do. It is like any other practice (e.g. riding a bike, playing the piano, or any other sport). It is not easy, but you get better each day with practice and consistency.

---

[9] https://www.pnas.org/content/116/37/18357

Positive Versus Negative Self -Talk

It may sound self-explanatory, but obviously, *positive* self-talk makes you feel *good* about yourself, and *negative* self-talk makes you feel *bad* about yourself… but it's even more than that. Good, optimistic, helpful self-talk makes you feel good about so many things in your environment. It makes you feel good about the things you have going on in your life, the ways you can contribute to the world, your accomplishments and milestones, your strengths and wins; it raises your vibration, and it makes you feel like nothing can stop you. It keeps you vibing high and is pretty much like an inner voice that tells you "GO, GO… you can do anything!" *Who doesn't want that?!*

Negative self-talk makes you feel low, angry, tired, low-vibe, and even when you have so many things to be grateful for you do not see the bright side of anything. Negative self-talk is often finite and overgeneralized in nature, and might sound like: "Everything is crap," or "This will never get better," or "My life sucks," or "I am so bad at this." Negative self-talk enjoys playing with the recency effect[10]; if one recent thing happened that was bad, your brain makes you exaggerate this one mishap and turn it into "everything is awful." This kind of thinking can be cyclical and can cause you to get stuck in that negative cycle if you aren't careful.

Over time, if you allow this level of talk to perpetuate, your negative self-talk may become your default mode. You find yourself picking up on negativity and stewing on the one bad thing in a sea of good things. You post something on social media and out of 20 excited comments, one person is negative and you allow yourself to focus on that one person. You ask your colleagues for their opinion on your new project, and even though eight people are on board with your ideas, you focus on those two people who gave you negative feedback. It can perpetuate and become your default mode if you aren't careful. If you experience negative self-

---

[10]The recency effect is the tendency to remember the most recently presented information best. https://www.verywellmind.com/the-recency-effect-4685058

talk too much, you could risk experiencing symptoms associated with depression[11] and it will likely be more difficult for you to be a happy and positive person again. This is why it's imperative for you to tackle this now, because the more work you put into this preventatively, the better and more positive your default self-talk will be. When your self-talk is positive, your self-esteem will elevate, you will make better choices in life, and you are more likely to crush your exercise plan and your goals in general.

You might be thinking that this is hard, and that because you have been doing it for your entire life — you are screwed. No, you are not screwed. I did it and I went deep. Positive self-talk brought me out of my negativity hole. Positive self-talk was the only way to overcome so many things in my life, not only my health. The thing about adjusting the dial on your self-talk gauge is that it has the potential to have an immediate effect. It can produce an instant shift in mindset and is something you can start implementing and incorporating on a daily basis — starting NOW. You don't have to wait for any circumstances to line up, for someone to give you permission, or for any prerequisites to be fulfilled. You can start changing how your internal dialogue functions TO-DAY. How cool is that?!

Here's the thing: **you are not a victim anymore**. You have the power inside of you. You have your WHY, and you are going to end your excuses right now and start changing your life. Do you believe that? I do, but I'm not responsible for your beliefs. Just like your internal dialogue, only **you** can decide that you believe you have the power inside you to change your life. You are going to stop telling yourself right now that you can't. You are going to start taking action because you only live once — and you can do this.

Now you know how to make a change, and you can start by no longer talking poorly to yourself. What good does it do — and

---

[11]Always speak with your doctor or healthcare professional when dealing with negativity and any other symptoms associated with depression.

what purpose does it serve — to keep that negative soundtrack playing? Stop putting yourself down. You are a **miracle** and you deserve to live happily and healthily. No more failed attempts. Today is the day you start saying nice things to yourself and stop making excuses about getting started. *Man, writing this just got me SO fired up!* This is the kind of stuff that we need to tell ourselves in order to conquer anything we want.

Aren't you fired up, too? Good! Let's talk about how you can start right now. From now on, you need to monitor yourself. Become a conscious observer of what's going on in your mind. Practice awareness of what thoughts are circulating in your head. If you've never done this before, you are likely not used to paying attention to what your thoughts are doing; they just… happen. It's time to start noticing. Imagine you are the "bad talk" police. It might sound funny to you, but it's true. You need to freaking *listen to your thoughts* and challenge the ones that are perpetually negative. You need to identify if you are mostly positive or mostly negative. I suggest that you use a journal to take specific notes and detail what you are thinking so that you can analyze it further and start to shift any thoughts that don't serve you.

You are going to be surprised by all of the crappy things you tell yourself. It can be harsh, and a tough pill to swallow, to realize just how mean and nasty you have been to yourself. Imagine if someone else was telling you the things you think about yourself. I bet you would be pretty unimpressed with that person, and my guess is that you'd likely forfeit future opportunities to spend time with someone who does nothing but put you down. Am I right? It is amazing to me how harsh we can be to ourselves, and we don't even notice it. When I think about my past, it often makes me upset, because I can recall the massive amounts of negative self-talk I allowed inside my head — about my image, body, food, abilities — it was astronomical. This is the reason that

I decided to write this book. I want to reach as many people as I can to tell them that all they need to do is be nice to themselves, and like Bob Marley says…*"every little thing, is gonna be alright."*

Challenge Your *"No Bueno"* Self -Talk

Challenging your *"no bueno"* self-talk is one of the most important things you can do that has exceptional power to change your health, and your life. When you begin to realize how much crap you have been telling yourself — without even knowing it — you are going to be able to compartmentalize the fact that, sometimes, you're your own worst enemy. Actually, most of the time, you're your own worst critic.

The first thing you need to do is to listen and be aware of what your inner voice is saying. Your inner voice is that daily monologue of thoughts that go directly to your subconscious mind, and in this case, we will look for all the negative ones. You will undoubtedly have positive ones as well, but I want you to pay close attention to the negative ones that you collect about your health, your body, and your eating habits. Those are the ones that I want you to focus on for now.

Over the next two days, I want you to carry this book with you everywhere you go. Use the space provided to write down some of your thoughts that you notice throughout that period of time. Particularly, pay attention to when you think something about yourself, your skills, your abilities, or your traits. I highly recommend that you do this periodically as a check-in with yourself, even after you do it for the first two days, because your thoughts will change every day, and this exercise will help you to see your progress with some tangibility.

Don't stress if you start with a bunch of negative and less-than-ideal internal thoughts. Unfortunately, it is common for your "default mode" self-talk to be more negative, so you're in good company. But we're also here to shift the narrative. The goal is to start to switch to more positive, high-vibe, self-serving thoughts, instead of self-sabotaging ones. Hopefully, when you read them again in the future, you will be so proud and happy that those thoughts are gone and *finito*[12] forever.

You may be unsure of what constitutes a thought to write down on the following pages. Here's an example: you make a tiny mistake (say, you start leaving your home and realize that you forgot to lock the front door, turn off the coffee machine, or feed the dog) and when you realize it, the first thing that comes to mind is *Ugh, I am SO stupid! I forgot to _____ AGAIN!* At first glance, you likely would not think twice about it. It happens, i*nside your head*, and it isn't hurting anyone else — so who cares? I care. This is not a good habit to allow. This is why it's necessary to take inventory of what's happening in your head on a daily basis. If you walk by the mirror and *think* *Eww, gross,* then that's something that you should track. If you answer a question in front of your boss and colleagues and then think: *That was awful, I suck at speaking in front of people*...TRACK IT.

You may be surprised at how often your hundreds of thoughts per day have a more negative tone, versus how often they have a more positive tone. Track them both. It may seem silly, unimportant, or, as mentioned previously, like it isn't hurting anyone, so why bother... but you should absolutely take the time to become aware, and then work to shift the energy around the thoughts that you have on a daily basis. If someone else were saying these things to you, it would hurt. You wouldn't dare give this kind of feedback to anyone you love — or, honestly, anyone you just KNOW, even if you don't have a strong relationship with them. *Why continue to say them to yourself?*

---

[12] Finito: If you know Italian then you most definitely know this. Meaning...it's finished. It's over. Bye bye bad self-talk. Forever. Adios!

Okay, so now you might be thinking, *how do I challenge these negative thoughts?* Well, I'm glad you asked. We will be doing a simple exercise that you can put into practice each time you feel the need to recharge the energy of your thoughts. Are you ready for this? It's really mind-blowing. The next time you think something negative *(I'm SO stupid!)* ask yourself…**Is there any actual evidence for what I'm thinking?**

This can relate to the catalogue of negative thoughts that you worked through previously, or to the kinds of limiting/finite statements that you often tell yourself.

For example:

I can never say NO to a delicious pastry or sweet.
Instead: Is this actually true? Is there evidence to support that this is 100% factual? Or am I exaggerating and blanketing this statement?

I only live once, and I need to enjoy and eat anything I want.
Instead: Is this actually true? Am I able to live my life and enjoy it without leaning so heavily on how food makes me feel? Have I ever seen evidence that I enjoyed my life/experiences without the need to eat or drink excessively?

Now that you're getting into the habit of being aware of your self-talk and limiting thoughts, you might be able to simply ask yourself this question (out loud or in your head). It should help you move through the thought and reframe it in a better way. It will help you to logically see that not everything you think has the validity of a true, actual fact. Some things tend to be taken as fact, but in reality, they are subjective and up to interpretation.

Is there any *actual* evidence for what I'm thinking? Is it *actually* true, or have I *made it seem* true? As you become aware of the things going through your head and begin trying to challenge your thoughts, my guess is that you're going to say *no, there isn't always evidence/truth/fact to the thought*. Now you challenge yourself to pick something healthier without hesitation. That's how I want you to challenge your thoughts from now on. Just because you think something doesn't automatically make it valid. You make them true or false; you make them penetrate into your conscious mind, and, similarly, **you now have the knowledge and power to change it.**

The next question that I want you to consider is: ***What would I say if a friend were in a similar situation?*** This question functions as a way to make you think critically about how you speak to yourself. We often care more about our loved ones than we do about ourselves, and consequently, we treat ourselves and our loved ones accordingly. If my sister or my friend were in the same situation as me and I heard how they were speaking to themselves, my first reaction would always be one of support, positivity, kindness, and grace. I would not berate my friend or my sister about how they made a mistake, how their appearance changed, or how they didn't present themselves the way they wanted to. I would be helpful, kind, and friendly. I would reaffirm positive things for them without hesitation. Sadly enough, if you are not paying attention to how you think and speak, you don't do this for yourself. Challenge your negative thoughts. **You are as important as your loved ones.**

The last question that I want you to ask yourself when you identify those negative thoughts is: ***Can I do anything to change what I am feeling bad about?*** Good news, *mis amigos!* The answer to this question is (nearly 100% of the time) *absolutely freaking YES!*

There is always an opposing law; good and bad, full and empty, tall and short, happy and sad — you name it. There is always a bright side and a flip side. Remember that. Challenge your thoughts in the same way. I recommend using your journal until you master this. Observing and comparing is my favourite part of the process, and I think it will quickly become one of your favourite things to do, too.

Positive Self-Talk, Positive Results

As easy as it sounds, it is not. If it were that easy, the world would be a better and happier place. Imagine if everybody were living in their perfect reality, healthy and happy! It would be amazing! And while this is certainly not an *easy* or *simple* task... it is not *impossible*. Everybody is capable of making simple, small changes that have the power to change their lives, but not many will execute. You and only *you* can change things for yourself; you just need to activate your discipline and internal willpower. Everything is possible when you decide to take action and work toward your goal. Now that you know the root of the problem, it is so much easier to tackle and get things done.

Make room for optimism. I know it is not easy to be perfectly *optimistic* all the time, but always remember that there is a reason and a learning opportunity in everything you experience. I say optimism because there is such a thing as toxic positivity,[13] and that's not what I'm trying to suggest to you here. I know that there are difficult experiences in life. As humans we go through hard things, and we have a wide array of emotions that often require processing. Not all of them will be good all the time, but if you want to have a better quality of life — and, in this case, to change your body, change your health, live longer, and spend the rest of your life away from the doctor — then this is it. You start by shifting your thoughts, and the more you establish positive thinking principles, the more peace you will begin to attract.

I am going to give you a few things that you can practice so that

---

[13] Toxic positivity is the belief that no matter how dire or difficult a situation is, people should maintain a positive mindset. It's a "good vibes only" approach to life. While there are benefits to being an optimist and engaging in positive thinking, toxic positivity instead rejects difficult emotions in favor of a cheerful, often falsely positive, facade. https://www.verywellmind.com/what-is-toxic-positivity-5093958#:~:text=Toxic%20positivity%20is%20the%20belief,vibes%20only%22%20approach%20to%20life.

you can exist more often inside of a more positive state of mind. You will want to consider doing these things daily. I can almost guarantee that you will feel a difference, and once you are there, you won't want to go back. Many successful, happy, and positive people do at least one of these methods each day. So why don't you try it, too? If you already practice it you will totally agree with me. It is easy and costs zero *dinero*.[14]

Numero Uno: The first practice is praying. I do not know what your beliefs are, but it doesn't matter. This is not specific to any particular religion; you simply need to believe in a higher power at play. To you, this could be a "source," the universe, God, etc. This is the most beautiful thing in the world. It will help you express thankfulness when things are going well, or whenever you feel something is not working, you can pray about the experience in order to find some lesson inside of it. Praying is the best therapy and will almost instantly calm your mind. Being able to pray is a blessing. When you pray you are communicating with a higher power, and I strongly believe that your higher power solves anything you are praying for.

Numero Dos: The second practice is gratitude. *You already knew this one, huh?* Right, but the question is: do you practice being grateful for the things in your life *every day?* Gratefulness brings more positivity to your life. When you're grateful, it's almost physically impossible to focus on the negative, on what you are missing, or your frustrations. It's very difficult for the brain to process both negative and positive emotions, so by implementing the strategy of gratitude, your brain has no choice but to focus on the positive. There is always something to be grateful for. Right this moment, you can be grateful for the fact that you are breathing while reading this book, that you have clean water in your fridge, or the simple fact that your heart is beating every day and keeping you alive. I encourage you to practice gratitude ev-

---

[14] money

ery day and write down in your journal things that you are grate-ful for. It can be the delicious cozy cup of coffee you drank this morning or that chat with your best friend. Gratefulness comes in many forms.

Numero Tres: This one is easy and you can do it while you are doing other things like driving, cooking, or walking around your neighbourhood. Listen to motivational videos, your favourite song, or recorded self-image that you created at the beginning of this book. This will help divert your mind to the positive and will raise your vibration.

Your inner dialogue is one of the most important things that you need to shift in order to have a better life. It is no one else's fault that you may have conditioning or pre-programming that has led you to a more negative "default mode." However, no matter what stage you are in currently, you need to stop and analyze your be-liefs and all of the crazy things that you keep telling yourself.

Back in my teenage years, my inner dialogue made me have the wrong idea about health. I hurt my body, my family, my relation-ships, and my parents. I planted a myriad of negative words in my subconscious mind, and I did it so often that I believed them wholeheartedly. No one told me to do and believe all of those things. I created all of them in my own mind, and over time, they rooted themselves in there at great depths.

In life, we are all shifting through different stages at varying paces. We each experience different people around us, different books and other materials, and different experiences — both good and bad — that have the power to teach us many things. There are always circumstances at play, but you do not need to continue to be a victim of circumstance. Start changing the way you look at things, start being kinder to yourself, and be kinder to others. You are so powerful and unique. You are a miracle, and you are here for a reason. Find that reason and live life to its fullest, the healthiest way you can. Celebrate life by nourishing and taking care of yourself.

In a Perfect World

Imagine how beautiful our world would be if everybody had the tools and resources to create the life they wanted to live in, inside the healthiest environment possible. Sounds amazing, right? The truth is that anyone can create the life they want, but it does take discipline. It takes time, studying, and practice. The key word is TIME. Do not expect to switch all of your bad habits and paradigms in a week. You must keep going, keep practicing, keep doing the work, and keep talking to yourself in a positive and kind way every day. Be your own best cheerleader, and **do not QUIT.** The worst thing you can do is quit on your dreams. I think that is the number one reason that a lot of people live an average life and just go with the flow, allowing anything and everything to just "happen." They quit too soon, and they expect any change they desire to happen fast. When it doesn't, they are disappointed and quit again. The cycle continues.

People talk themselves out of their own dreams. Life and events happen and they forget what they are fighting for. It is not easy, but it is not impossible. Do not punish yourself if you fail at something. No one is perfect! Press that reset button and do it again, until you get better and better. Do not quit! Always go back to your goal and your motivation. You only live once and you deserve to feel healthy, energetic, and happy every day.

The thing is, when it comes to the kind of work I'm explaining inside these pages, most people will make one of two assumptions: either they think it is too simple, or too difficult. The former may think it is not worth their time, so they don't attempt it. People in this category would think or say things like, *"Why should I bother with gratitude? What could writing down what I'm grateful for possibly have to do with making changes in my life?"* Or, *"Why should I bother with this **Power Health Self** script? What is repeating that every day going to do for me?"* They have likely never tried either of the two practices in question, but they're quick to write it off because they don't understand how they could possibly create results. The other type of person will think the things I'm asking you to do in this book are quite the opposite: they think the practices are too difficult. These people will think and say things like, *"I don't have time to write out some crazy 'script' about my new life."* Or *"I hardly have time to grocery shop...I couldn't possibly add anything else to my morning routine; I'm already swamped."* They make up the belief that these simple practices are too *hard* to implement, that they are too much extra work, and that they couldn't possibly add these tasks into their lives on a daily basis. It's either too simple or too hard.

If you're someone who has fallen into one of these two categories, you'll know it by one simple test: did you complete the journal exercise I asked you to do when you started reading this book? Have you created your new **Power Health Self** script yet? Did you write out all of your old paradigms? Is every journal activity completed so far, or did you skip over those sections with an eye roll and a quick page skim?

If you didn't complete the activities and you're reading this now, don't worry. Nobody will ever know. You can dog-ear or place a bookmark in this page, go back to the journaling section, and fill in all of the exercises as they were meant to be filled in. I will never know. But what I would like you to consider is how many times in your life you have written off something that you hadn't yet tested or experienced simply because you had already made a decision or an assumption about it. This is your opportunity to change gears. This is your opportunity to make big changes with simple practices. If you haven't tried these things before, now is your chance to take a step down a brand new path and see what comes to fruition for you.

...and if you already did all the exercises as instructed at the outset...good job, my friend! Keep moving forward!

One of the things that helped me the most when I was struggling on my health journey was studying more about my body. If you research and read about the anatomy of the human body, you will discover that your body is a true marvel of engineering. It starts from the smallest of atoms that regenerate to become molecules. Those molecules create cells, which create tissues. Those tissues create organs. Organs create body systems. Your body systems literally make you who you are and keep you alive. Your body works 24 hours a day, seven days a week. It is operating involuntarily, non-stop. It keeps you breathing, keeps your heart beating, processes your food and water for you, regulates your temperature, helps you think, helps you see and hear all the beautiful sights and sounds in the world, helps you to lift and carry things, and even helps women *create new humans!* Your body never takes a vacation; it is permanently indebted to you and functions only to serve you as you go through life.

When I realized how miraculous my body was, I felt guilty. I had mistreated it. I didn't eat on purpose in order to be "skinny," I punished myself mentally and stressed my body with the wrong circumstances. When you realize how big of a miracle you are, you will feel the need to take care of your being. Do not let health or other circumstances let you get to that point at which you can't value your existence and the temple that is your body.

There is only one you. There is only one you that has your unique purpose on this planet. There is only one you that can bring joy to your family, to your kids, and to your parents. There is only one chance to BE YOU. There is only one chance to live to your fullest, and there is only one chance to run this marathon called life. Don't you dare waste it. If you are running a marathon, you might as well make it powerful, joyful, and inspiring. Do it for you and no one else. Do it so you wake up every morning *so freaking excited* to be alive and to live another day healthy, giving so much joy, inspiration, and good to others.

The world needs more people like that. The world would be a better place if we just changed our attitudes and decided to live our lives in the most powerful way possible. Aspire to be the person who inspires other people to become better each day. Everybody has ups and downs, and we all have the same 24 hours in a day. Use them effectively. Take every challenge as a learning experience, **but do not quit.** Capitalize on positive life experiences that fill up your tank, and then spread that happiness with more people. You have the power inside of you. You are a miracle, and everything you touch and do for others becomes a miracle.

Keep Paying Attention

Remember to watch and be aware of what you tell yourself. You have already worked to identify those negative thoughts. Learn to get into the habit of replacing them with positivity, and then practice, practice, practice. You need to do this with consistency so that you can rewire the thought patterns inside your brain. You already have the basic tools that you need to change your health. Now there are no excuses. Go back and read the chapters again if you need to. When you feel down, read these pages again. Let me be there for you and support you on your journey. Repeat this declaration to yourself: **"I am mindful and aware of things that affect my wellness; I only choose to read, listen to, and interact with positive and uplifting things, because I am a miracle and I deserve to feel happy and healthy."**

You are in the process of reprogramming your mind, and your body is going to respond to anything you tell yourself, both externally and internally. Self-talk is a powerful tool connecting your mind and body, and you must use this connection to your benefit.

In the next chapter, we are going to talk about your experiences. You now know how to create experiences with your own mind through repetition, visualization, and changing your self-image. Those things are going to give you the power to take **action** to change your health. Your body and overall health status will change when you *do* something. You can't *just think* about doing something; you must also *move toward it.* Real experiences will give you the power to stick to a plan, feel confident, and love your new healthy life. You can have the best personal trainer, the best gym, and the best nutritionist — but if your mind and self-image are not ready for change, you won't go the distance or stick to the plan for long. The next chapter is going to help you generate ideas for how to create real experiences that will initiate your journey and then, subsequently, keep you going down the right path. Remember, **you and only you** have the power to do this, and I believe in you 100%!

Part 2:

Change Your Mind, Change Your Life

"

Create experiences in your mind, and they will come to life in your reality.

"

- Tdachi-Deni Whiting

Chapter 5:
Your Experiences Are the Keys to Success

Earlier when we were talking about your self-image, I mentioned that the brain can't differentiate between what is real and what is not real. The power of your imagination is amazing. One of the most underutilized tools humans have at our disposal is the use of visualization. You can use your imagination to create your preferred version of reality. You can act like you are already that healthy, invincible person with great habits; that fit, healthy and *so freaking happy and joyful person*, enthused with life and operating with the mentality that nothing can stop you. You already worked on that part.

I know you are working on visualizing the way you want things to be in your life, and this is a key component to making that happen. But now it is time to discuss *real* experiences, not imaginary ones. In my personal experience this was the hardest part, because when you visualize things, you aren't necessarily on the hook for executing or rationalizing the pictures in your mind. When we're talking about real-life experiences, now is the time to go out there, be brave, and take action. No more hiding...*now* is the time where everything you have been putting into practice has to take form in real life.

When you are working toward bettering your health, it is essential that you put all of these new habits and your new **Power Health Self** into action. This is the only way to change your body and your health. Just as the only logical way to shape your body and change its composition is by putting it under stress (exercising) and lowering your calorie intake so that your metabolic rate changes, taking action is how we make the visualizations come to life. This is where the magic happens. If you want to change your life and change your body, you must take action to do so. Taking action is *required* in order to ignite change.

Do not panic! It might sound a little scary, but I can promise you that this is the best part of all. Throughout this process, you are going to experience and discover so many things about yourself, including how much power you have within.

Experience is how you perceive the world around you. You have the ability to decide how you would like to feel. Experience helps you to know *how your desired outcome feels,* and in this case, you want to know how it feels to be "next-level" healthy. You need to get out of your comfort zone and take action. You need to put on your workout clothes, tie your shoes, and GO. You need to say *no mas*[15] to all of those sugary drinks, and say *yes* to more nutritious, whole foods. You need to know how living healthy feels, because it is freaking awesome to be able to: feel energized, run easily without getting winded, put on your clothes and be happy they fit, live a longer and happier life because your health is so awesome that you don't have any pain or have to visit your doctor, and more! You need to experience how it feels and what it looks like *for you.* Once you are there, I promise you will refuse to go back.

Creating these experiences is not very hard, because we are humans — and when we are excited for something, nothing can stop us. The most difficult part is consistency, but we've discussed that already. We are going to work through creating healthier habits together that will in turn create the results you desire.

Now you have the right tools and you know that **you create what**

---

[15] This means "no more."

you are with what you constantly think about, you can start to change your reality from the inside out. You now know that your internal dialogue is so important, and that you must shift the energy of your self-talk in order to uplift your mind and body. You now know that, every time you create an excuse to do something that is not bringing you closer to your goal, you are going to read your big goal over and over again and remind yourself of your "why." As you've already established, this goal includes your burning desire. This goal will become your main focus, even when you start to slip and need to hit the reset button.

You must take small steps, with consistency. You must crawl before you can run. I am not suggesting that you should drop everything else in your life, show up at the gym tomorrow, and then run a marathon next week. You will take baby steps, because while mind and body changes are often quite simple, this work is not necessarily *easy.*

The first thing you need to decide is what baby steps you can begin to do to create a real experience that mirrors how you'll feel when you reach your goal. You could start by obtaining some workout clothes, going for a walk with your dog each day, or maybe doing a workout at home where no one can see you so you feel more comfortable. You can choose to say no to the fast food that your kids are constantly requesting and decide to cook something healthy at home instead. Yes, those small adjustments to your experiences count. Even though you are not yet completing or accomplishing your big, long-term goal yet, these baby steps are actually quite massive to check off while you are working toward what it is that you really desire.

These baby steps are going to build your competence and confidence levels, release dopamine that elicits feelings of happiness, and make you feel good about yourself. The more experiences you can cultivate that bring you positive results, the better. Momentum will build and small, sustainable progress over time will help you to realize that what you thought was hard isn't that hard at all. You will be confident that you can accomplish more, and you will keep going.

I want to remind you now about the power of affirmations, visualizations, positive self-talk, and self-image practices. These habits are huge when you start creating your experiences. This is why I talk about the power of all of these things at the beginning of the book — because they are so important. Without these things, you might not create any experiences, because you might keep telling yourself you can't, or make any excuse you want so you do not accomplish anything. Truthfully, it's easier to be stagnant, and if you don't do anything, you'll just stay where you are. Excuses are easier to create than change. They require literally zero effort and can be completed with the speed of instant gratification. They require no outside-the-box thinking, no new habits, and no potentially difficult work. Make sure you remember to keep thinking and telling yourself positive things, listening to your self-image script, and always going back to review your goals. These tools won't let you down; these tools will give you the superpowers to accomplish anything you want and give you the real-life experiences you need to live in order to completely change your old, *no bueno,* unhealthy self-image.

One of the hardest parts will undoubtedly be to complete the daily practice, but please know: you deserve to be healthy because you are a miracle, and you deserve the best happy and healthy life that you want. Evaluate where you are each day. When you feel down, write your affirmations, play your favourite song, create simple movements to raise your vibration and shift your energetic state, because these simple things will help to remind you that you are unstoppable. Visualize regularly; it will take you to your happy place and has the potential to change your vibration level as well. When you feel down, ask yourself: *Who do I have to become in order to receive and feel all of the things I want in life?* I cannot stress this enough. Your mind is either your best friend or your worst enemy, so use it intelligently and with purpose.

Affirm What You Want to Achieve

So far you have been working hard at rewiring your beautiful mind. You've identified your paradigms and excuses, you've created your new **Power Health Self**, you've set some excellent short and long-term goals, and, hopefully, you're starting to feel good about the direction you're going in.

Now, I want to talk a little more about affirmations. Maybe you've heard of them, seen them posted on social media, or maybe you are reading this and you're like *I live by affirmations. I do them every day!* In that case, amazing! Keep it up!

If you haven't heard about them, no worries. Affirmations are powerful tools we humans can use to practice positive thinking, empower ourselves, and maintain a high vibrational energy. Affirmations are positive statements formatted in the present tense, and they're really simple to use and implement into your life. In order for them to have the most impact, you need to repeat them to yourself frequently throughout the day.

To be effective you need to choose your affirmations wisely. They must be created according to what you want to **become or achieve.** You can either write them down or say them out loud to yourself. Some people do this practice while looking at themselves in the mirror. I will be honest with you — I thought this idea was silly at first. I felt awkward when I did it for the first time in front of the mirror. As I spoke, looking directly into my own eyes in the mirror, I was cringing. My mind was like, *what the heck are you doing?* But I knew it was my old paradigm. I knew it was something new that my mind was rejecting by default. I had never seen somebody do this personally, so it felt weird. But I persevered, and I'm so glad that I gave it another chance. I kept going, and I must tell you — when you look at yourself **directly in the eye** in the reflection of that mirror, while saying these things to yourself — it is so freaking powerful.

I kept going, saying all of these affirmations that I created surrounding all that I wanted to be and become. It is so powerful! You get so freaking fired up! With regular practice, you will begin to believe the things you're saying, and you'll feel your body shifting energy. Your vibration is so high that you will get a natural super-boost after doing this. It is okay to feel weird in the beginning. Everything new feels that way anyway, so why not give it a try?

The good news is that you do not have to do it in front of the mirror if you do not want to. You can use pen and paper or simply put them on audio. The main thing is that you need to create this affirmation based on what you want to change in your life; on what you want your beautiful being to feel and be.

One of the simplest ways that you can begin to create and incorporate your own, unique, personalized affirmations is to go back to the activity we did on paradigms and excuses. You can take your existing, conditioned paradigms, beliefs, and excuses and completely rewrite them in the form of affirmations, so that you can start the process of believing the opposite of your old excuses. These affirmations rewire your mind, raise your energy, and create real experiences that will help your mind feel more confident. You will rewrite your excuses into a positive affirmation in the present tense, and repeat for as many of your old beliefs as you'd like.

You are going to sort that list and ask yourself, *which of these excuses, bad habits, or doubts are holding me back from becoming* my **Power Health Self?** Pick one or two from that list, and re-member that you can always add more any time you want. We will be working with these paradigms for three weeks at a time, and after three weeks, we will add one or two more.

For example:

Old paradigm/belief: *I do not sleep at night. I never have energy!*

Your affirmation becomes: *My body and mind are always ready to rest. I am always energized!*

Or maybe you're thinking: *This is bullsh*t! How can this possibly change me? This is so stupid!*

Your affirmation becomes: *I am open to change. This is new in-formation, and I open my heart and my mind to better my health and my life.*

This is not a fairy tale. This is real. I am not inventing this tech-nique, and I am not the only one who has had a positive, trans-formational experience with affirmations. Many people use this method on a regular basis. It is a powerful thing, and if you hav-en't tried it before, I invite you to open your heart and your mind. Do not take this information for granted.

JOURNAL EXERCISE:

Go back to your list of all of the excuses and paradigms that you created on page 36 and pick two things that you want to work on the most. When you have picked the ones that you want to work with, write them down in the space provided below. Then, rewrite them as a positive, present-tense statement. You can record them and play them while you are exercising, driving, or doing the dishes, or you can even write them on sticky notes and paste them in different places where you can easily read them any chance you have.

(I highly recommend you record them. This is easier to do, and you can repeat them any place you want, at any time you want.)

Old Paradigm:

_____

New Affirmation:

_____

Old Paradigm:

_____

New Affirmation:

_____

Do Not Punish Yourself

What do I mean when I say "punish yourself?" Self-punishment is quite a common phenomenon in our society. It has been proven and documented in various studies that self-punishment reduces feelings of guilt.[16] It doesn't matter what topic you are talking about; when you think you did something wrong, you will punish yourself with words, or, in extreme cases, physically and emotionally. Your mind is the GPS of pretty much everything around you — and all that you attract into your life. Guilt can prevent you from enjoying life and thriving emotionally. I have lived many different scenarios in my life in which I punished myself for little things, and I bet you have too.

Self-punishment relieves accumulated feelings that you are not proud of, but it can impact how others perceive you as well. When I had my eating disorder, I used to punish myself both physically and mentally, by starving myself and inciting harmful self-talk. If I ate more than I was supposed to (according to nobody but me) or if I ate that cake that I believed I shouldn't have eaten at my friend's birthday party, my internal dialogue would then immediately default to something like: *Deni, what have you done?! You are so weak. You are fat. You shouldn't be eating cake. Go exercise for an hour so you can burn off what you ate.*

I was constantly monitoring my actions and behaviours and analyzing them inside my head as good or bad. If I resisted eating "forbidden" food, I was good. If I gave in to what I thought was a treat/temptation (cake at a party, drinks at an event) then I was bad. Nobody else could hear what was going on inside my head. Nobody else knew I was punishing myself with words and with avoiding food altogether, but I was doing it constantly. This is truly *self*-punishment.

This constant expression of self-punishment made that part of

---

[16]By practicing self-punishment, we ease our feelings of guilt, free our conscience, and allow ourselves to re-engage in life. Self-punishment tends to serve a dual purpose, as it not only relieves internal feelings of guilt, but impacts how others perceive us as well. https://www.psychologytoday.com/us/blog/the-squeaky-wheel/201407/why-do-we-punish-ourselves

my life Hell. Nothing was more important than my obsession about not eating and being so focused on my body and what I ate, avoided, or how long I worked out to "make up" for being "bad." I told myself so many negative things, regularly called myself names, cut myself off from people I cared about, neglected my physical needs, and punished my mind and body every day. I felt lonely, desperate and depressed. The sad part is that I realize now that I did it to myself. No one else put me through that bad experience; It was my thoughts, my words, my self-talk, and my self-punishment.

I wanted to touch on this topic because I feel it is so important for you to know and consider. It is okay to experience failure and not be perfect on your health journey. It is okay to have cake that your coworker brought to the office for her birthday. It is okay if one day you just want to be in your comfy yoga pants and just sit all day and eat popcorn until you cannot eat anymore. IT IS OKAY! There are so many circumstances that could happen in your life, and you really need to become an expert at listening to what your body and mind need at all times. Sometimes, you may plan to do a workout but instead realize that you need some Netflix and chill time. Sometimes, you have a great, healthy day filled with lots of water, veggies, and protein sources, and then you feel like having a bowl of ice cream with your family after dinner. When you're operating with a health-focused mindset, you know that when you have things you might consider "treats" in moderation, they really don't make that much of a difference long-term. It becomes an issue if you're having ice cream after every meal every single day. That's not ideal, but neither is eating the same exact healthy meals every day of your life — though you'd be eating "healthy" food, you'd be SO BORED and you'd be missing out on a ton of other valuable nutrients and minerals provided by a **variety** of healthy foods, not just the same ones over and over.

Finding a way to create a balanced, healthy lifestyle will be so rewarding for you! The benefits are long-term and have massive advantages. You need to find a way to live a healthy *lifestyle,* not just commit to a short-term or temporary healthy "program." You need **balance** in your life. You can't be perfect and productive all the time. No one in this world can hold everything together all the time!

I want you to know this because I have heard so many times from my clients and friends that they feel they've "ruined everything" when they make one little mistake or have one little bad experience. It often leads to self-punishment, and that never ends well. You feel stuck, you go against yourself, you feel defeated, embarrassed, and out of control. Does that sound familiar? Of course — everybody does this at some point in their life. I am here to remind you that this pattern is not constructive or helpful; you are a valuable human, and you are allowed to live a life in which you are focused on health. You prioritize it for yourself, but you realize that nobody is perfect, life is full of moderation, and you aren't going to "ruin everything" just because you decided to grab a cookie with your coffee.

As humans, we have an innate desire to feel connected and accepted (by others). As a result, we often think that we need to shape ourselves to be "perfect" so that we can be accepted, but life happens, and it will never be perfect. Sometimes you are going to fail and sometimes you are going to succeed; sometimes you are going to be accepted by people and sometimes you won't. And that, *mis amigos,* is okay!

When you are aware of this energy, you won't attract anything good. It most likely will convert into anxiety, depression, or anger. So the question is, how do you liberate yourself from self-punishment? Well, the first step is to recognize it, and to understand that all of this punishment is affecting your self-esteem and goals.

You need to create a more positive environment for your mind by using positive self-talk and listening to your self-image script. This will improve your health and well-being, and of course bring you closer to your goals. At this point, you could either be thinking, *Hmm, I do not think I punish myself...* or you could be saying to yourself, *Man, I gotta stop being so hard on myself.* I am going to give you some examples that might help you if you are punishing yourself. Are you ready? Keep reading.

ASK YOURSELF THE FOLLOWING QUESTIONS:

*Circle Y or N at the end of each statement.

1. Are you overeating every time you feel stressed, sad, or depressed? **Y / N**

2. Are you refusing to ask for help when you need it? **Y / N**

3. Are you drinking or getting drunk to feel accepted or to help you forget the low or hard parts of that day? **Y / N**

4. Are you criticizing yourself, or telling yourself what an awful failure you are for doing something? **Y / N**

5. Are you giving up on your previously set goals because one day you did not get a result that you wanted, and you just told yourself, *"I am not good enough for this?"* **Y / N**

6. Are you under-eating because you think you are "fat?" **Y / N**

7. Are you saying yes to everything that comes up until you run yourself down? **Y / N**

8. Are you depriving yourself of sleep because you "need" to do more and be more productive? **Y / N**

9. Are you saying no to new opportunities because you think you are not good enough? **Y / N**

10. Are you quitting your workout classes because the first day you wanted to puke and felt like the loser of the class? **Y / N**

How many questions did you answer YES to, out of 10? If you answered yes to even 1 or 2 of these questions, you have a tendency to punish yourself. You deserve to live a better, healthier life. Now you have the key. You become what you think, and you have the power to change it. You *can* live in peace. You just have to do the work and be honest with yourself by becoming aware of, analyzing, and addressing your own self-punishment tendencies. Switch them and write down affirmations that assert the opposite. Remember, all of these pre-conditioned ideas are an existing part of you. You have them on repeat. Your unconscious mind memorizes and acts on them, so you have to delete them with the repetition of positive self-talk and your new image.

Identify What Makes You Happy

In life, people tend to always do what makes them happy or more comfortable. The comfortable road is the easier road. It's the paved road. It's the road without any speed bumps, potholes, or roadblocks. It's the road that has no twists or turns, and you could likely drive that road with your eyes closed because you've done it so much. But it's the easier road because it's the one you know best, and it doesn't challenge you in any way. It doesn't help you grow and change if it doesn't challenge you. The secret here is that you must find something that challenges you but also makes you *happy.*

If you do something that you aren't passionate about, or something that makes you unhappy, you will most likely not stick to it. If you are happy and comfortable doing something, there is nothing that will make you *not* do it. I always tell my clients that you cannot follow a random diet, or just do the same workout program that your best friend is so passionate about, because we are all different and we all like and dislike different things. There is no one way to move your body; there is no one way to eat a healthy diet; there is no one way to live a holistic lifestyle.

In order to succeed in your new power healthy life, you need to try and experience different things and see what will adapt more to your personality. When you follow a specific diet, your dietitian or your personal trainer should talk with you so they get to know your current diet and what you like or dislike. Also consider the fact that bodies are all so different, and that something traditionally "healthy" may not respond well to *your* unique body. You might eat tomatoes because they're healthy but don't pay attention to the fact that tomatoes give you heartburn. Why would you keep eating something "healthy" that doesn't respond well to your body? Alternatively, imagine your entire diet includes veggies that you don't even *like*. They're healthy, but you don't enjoy the taste of them. There is likely a zero percent chance that you are going to follow that diet. So, this is why trial and error and truly listening to your own body to find the correct path for you is so important. Even if the path is the road less travelled, it will be worth it.

If you, like many, are a naturally introverted person, and you are not very outgoing or are very shy, there is a very low chance that you will go to a gym or exercise class by yourself at the beginning of your journey. You might do better with some at-home workouts at first. Remember, you can change these paradigms by working on your self-image — but this process takes time. While you work on your new self-image, it is important that you select options in which you are going to feel more comfortable, so you can start creating real-life experiences that will bring you closer to your goals.

In the beginning of my fitness journey, I did not want anyone to see me struggling to run one mile on the treadmill. I didn't want anyone to see me sweating or be next to strangers when my confidence and self-esteem were very low. That was a reflection of my self-image during that time. What I did instead was work out at my house with my mom's old fitness DVDs. I remember in Mexico that there was a "healthy" cereal brand that came with exercise DVDs inside. I used to do those at home, in the comfort of my living room. They were really good, and they helped me gain confidence and bring new experiences to my life. Now, I can go anywhere and do any workout you could imagine. I am so passionate about moving that I do not care if people laugh at me. My self-image has adjusted and changed, and it allows me to move through life with confidence instead of concern. Look for options that align with your current self-image so you can start creating those real-life experiences that will bring you joy and excitement.

We are going to be doing a little test that will help you find options that go with your current personality or self-image. The most important thing here is that you start moving and take action. It doesn't matter if you start by simply walking your dog more often. You need to start creating real-life experiences with the new self-image you've created. This is the only way you will change your health and your habits. Working on your mind is great, but that alone won't get the job done. You need to start eating healthier and moving more, and you need to pick wisely so that you can start liking the process and being excited every time it is time to work on your health. I am going to give you a little exercise. It's going to be fun.

Personality Matters: Picking Your Fitness Path

When you start your exercise journey it can be overwhelming and emotional, especially if you haven't worked out in a while. It is important to identify where your feelings and your current self-image lie. This current self-image is the one that you are trying to improve by taking action, reprogramming your subconscious mind, and creating these awesome new experiences. Every single one of us carries a unique personality, and this is what defines us and makes us different from each other. Different aspects of our life define us, and I strongly believe that personality changes when self-image is altered. Right now you are working on it, and we need to adjust things so that your new journey to a healthier you is a success. You need to feel comfortable and happy, otherwise you will quit at some point.

I am going to help you identify what kind of workout can work for you at the beginning of this journey, so you can make a better choice in picking your path. You need to discover which path will work best for you right now while you work toward a healthier you.

I am not a psychologist and there might be many more personality categories, but we are going to focus on three. I believe that these categories will help us find a path where we can start right now and take action.

QUIZ #1
Be honest with your answers. Circle "YES" or "NO."

I enjoy working out with other people. **Y / N**

A little competition excites me and sets my
heart on fireeeeee. **Y / N**

I enjoy my trainer yelling, "Go faster! Go!" or
"You can squat lower than that!" **Y / N**

The more sweat the better! **Y / N**

I am adventurous. I love learning new things and
going to unknown places. **Y / N**

I want to beat my running time from the day before. **Y / N**

Okay. If you answered mostly **"YES"**
go to Result #1 on page 126. If you
answered mostly **"NO,"** go to Quiz #2.

QUIZ #2

Be honest with your answers. Circle "YES" or "NO."

If I am at a gym, I try to be like a ninja. I don't
want to bring too much attention to myself. **Y / N**

I feel more comfortable hanging out by myself and
achieving my goals without help from others. **Y / N**

I am never bored because I have myself to
keep me company. **Y / N**

Team challenge workout...mmmmm, No thanks! **Y / N**

I do not overthink my workouts. I do not need
assistance or supervision from anyone! **Y / N**

Friday night sounds like a bubble bath, Netflix,
and wine. **Y / N**

I am my own inner critic/cheerleader, who drives
me to meet my goals. **Y / N**

Okay. If you answered mostly **"YES"** go to Result #2 on page
126. If you answered mostly **"NO,"** go to Quiz #3.

QUIZ #3

Be honest with your answers. Circle "YES" or "NO."

I want to connect my mind and body, and do not care about my muscles. **Y / N**

True health means caring for the total being... my body and mind. **Y / N**

I love to align my energy at the beginning or end of the day. **Y / N**

I love connecting with my inner self. **Y / N**

Breathing and stretching my body is a must in my daily routine. **Y / N**

Slow movements and low impact are best for my body. **Y / N**

I love the relaxed and centered feeling I get from breathing and stretching my body. **Y / N**

Okay. If you answered mostly **"YES"**
go to Result #3 on page 127.

RESULT #1
You are outgoing, extroverted, energetic, socially interactive, and driven by emotional rewards, *mi amiga(o)*.

You are social and competitive. You prefer exercising with a team, friend, or personal trainer. You just put your blindfolds on and are able to easily reach the goals you set for yourself or your coach sets for you. You do not mind working out surrounded by people, and you are motivated by competition. You do not mind being sweaty and smelly around people, and your confidence is mostly pretty high. You might already be into the fitness world. Discipline is not an issue for you, but you perform better if someone is motivating you or keeping track of your goals. Your current self-image has driven you there. Maybe you are not into any fitness program yet, but this personality shows off at your work or at school.

You will be more attracted to free weights, endurance-based activities like biking, swimming, or even extreme hikes or rock climbing. You can try fitness meetups and fitness challenges. Goal-oriented workouts like boot camps, Zumba, and even races and marathons will fuel your motivation. Your heart and spirit will feel accomplished and happy when you are done with your workout. Go out there and join or try a class. I promise you this will set your soul on fire.

RESULT #2

You are an introvert and Solo Soul.
You can just be by yourself and do not want to be noticed. Talking to people and interacting with others while you work out feels uncomfortable to you. You are your own cheerleader, and you can set and achieve goals on your own without any help from trainers, coaches, or friends. You would rather work out at your

house where no one can see you because you are independent and disciplined. Your main goal is to move your body and get the health benefits of exercise most of the time, and one of your goals when you workout is to clear your head and release stress.

Endurance-based activities are good for you, like SOLO biking, running, walking, or even hiking. You will perform well with on-line workouts. Write down your favourite hobbies. You can go after work or school and do some exercise by yourself doing something you love.

RESULT #3
You are the Holistic and Yogi Type.

Your body is your temple. You most likely will enjoy exercising in an environment where you can focus on improving both your body and your mind. You can be an introvert or an extrovert. Slow and low impact movements are important to you. You think an efficient and short body and mind connection will bring you back to life, and you need this centering in your daily routine. You can try yoga, Pilates and Tai-Chi. These types of exercises will satisfy both your fitness and relaxation goals.

This fun quiz gives you an idea of what you can start doing in regard to movement that will align with your personality type. Your self-image will change with the exercises you are doing. If I look at my timeline, I was the shy, introverted one when I started my health journey. I did not want anybody to see me. But now it is another story. I will do pretty much any type of exercise alone or with a team.

It is up to you — and the power you give your mind and your self-image — to work toward your goal. In the next chapter, we will focus a little bit more on the importance of your health and how miraculous your body is. When I studied for my personal trainer certification it impacted me greatly, and my goal since that day has been to remind everybody how awesome and smart their bodies are. We often forget about it, and just exist and take for granted all that our body does for us every single day.

I remember very clearly when I was studying about the process it takes to digest a meal, while shoveling food into my mouth without chewing my food properly. After reading that, I literally wanted to smack myself. I always ate too fast, and I'm still working on it because it is a habit that I've had all my life. But now I value my body more, and I know that eating quickly doesn't help my digestive process very much. Now I am aware of the importance of chewing my food, and I am working on improving that habit. This is why I want to remind you of all of the miracles that happen 24/7 inside of you. This will make you appreciate your beautiful body and be aware each time you make a choice. My hope is that it will also make you feel so grateful for all it does for you.

66

*The human body
is the best work of art.*

99

- Jess C. Scott

Chapter 6: Amazing Things Your Body Does for You

I know you have probably taken an anatomy class at some point in your life, but maybe you were too young to realize or value how awesome and smart the human body is. We usually complain about our bodies based on the physical manifestation of it, compared to what we see around us or in advertising, marketing, movies, television, magazines, etc. Because of that, you might not like something about how your body looks. You might get angry when you are hungry, because the last thing you want to do is eat when you associate eating with how your body looks. Maybe you notoriously get a pimple before big important days and it makes you frustrated with your skin. A lot of us might have a long list of things that we dislike about our bodies, or we think or say we wish we had an aesthetic that we don't currently have: *I wish I had bigger boobs; I wish I had a bubble butt; I wish I had a flat stomach with visible abs.* You might be laughing right now because it is true — and unfortunately, it's especially true of women. Women are constantly looking at other women and wishing they had bodies like theirs.

My goal in this chapter is to show you that even though you may dislike or even despise some things about your body, your body is always there for you. No matter what you feed it, how you treat it, or what you put it through, your body is *always* there for you! It adapts, transforms, digests, heals itself, and allows you to walk, run, and jog. It allows you to hug. It lets you play with your kids. It allows you to rest and sleep, to enjoy different tastes and smells, and to speak, share, and connect with other people. It is your best friend — or at least, it should be! It will go and go until it cannot go anymore; it will go farther than even your mind thinks it will go. Your brain often gives up before your body does.

If you treat your body well with nutrient-dense food and regular exercise, your body will go far and last for a long time. If you do the opposite — if you feed it unhealthy, processed food on a regular basis and do not give it the movement it craves and deserves — your body is likely to get sick, break down, and potentially become filled with disease.

In this chapter, I want to show you all of the things that your body does while you eat, sleep, talk, watch TV, exercise, etc. I tweaked it a little bit so it won't get too boring for you. I will show you some of the awesome things that your body does for you, and at the same time, give you some facts about what is happening inside of you while this is all going on.

Your body has different levels of organization. There are multi-level organization systems that make your body function properly. It all starts with an atom, and these atoms combine to create molecules. The human body is composed of only six of them: oxygen, carbon, hydrogen, nitrogen, calcium, and phosphorus. The next level is the cellular level; these are miraculously organized and smart, and know what kind of tissues to form. Your tissues create muscle tissues that are part of your organs, and organs are what make up your body systems — your cardiovascular system, respiratory system, etc. And the grand finale is an organism: a human being. Stop right there! Please think about how your whole body starts from an atom and it becomes YOU. You are a freaking miracle. Your body is one of the smartest things that exists in the whole world; and to be honest, most of us take it for granted. We just exist; we do not think about how amazing our being is. We just live our lives without caring about our temple.

Earlier in my life, I was focused on having fun, fitting in with my friends, and getting drunk. I was not focused on giving my body the right nutrients. Some of my excuses were: *I only live once… If I die tomorrow, at least I enjoyed my life and did what I wanted.* I was so selfish that I didn't even care about the beauty and magnificence of my body. In my opinion, all of these were paradigms. The way I grew up, living life to the max meant not caring about my body and only caring about how I could fit in with others. I now know that living life to its fullest potential is so much more than that. Living my best life means that now my top priority is to be healthy, happy, and successful in achieving my goals.

I want you to think about some of the amazing functions that the body has. Thinking about this made me realize just how awesome and smart the human body is, and also the importance of taking care of it. I love telling my clients these things, because when you remind yourself about all of the things your body does for you, it makes you realize that life and health are more than being skinny and looking good.

Health is the absence of disease. Health is the condition of your mind. Health is taking care of your physical and mental health. Health is being there for all of the people you love, being energized, being in peace, being motivated, being without pain, being able to spend more days in this wonderful world, and enjoying all of the blessings that God made for us. Negativity, gossip, and stress won't make you a healthy person, and of course won't make you live a good life. We are going to start with my favourite part of the body. We will make this fun, and I will make this section like a little game. Grab your tea or coffee, paper, and pen, and keep reading. We are about to discover and go over all of the wonderful things that your body does.

The rule of the game is that throughout the next section, you need to write down in your journal the hidden **<u>bold, underlined</u>** words that you find. Make sure to write them down in order so that you can discover the message at the end. Ready? Let's do this!

1. Corazon - Your heart ♥

> "*The human heart beats approximately 4,000 times per hour and each pulse, each throb, each palpitation is a trophy engraved with the words 'you are still alive.' You are still alive. Act like it.*" - Rudy Francisco

I absolutely love this quote. Your heart is one of the most important muscles that you have. Your heart is a miracle, and it is magnificent. Your heart begins working before birth and continues to work until death. Your heart works less efficiently when it's bored and does not have too much to do. Isn't that funny? This is why it is important that you keep it busy and give it some cardiovascular exercise.

What have you done for your beautiful pumping heart lately? Have you given it some exercise? Something like running, skipping, HIIT training, or even a brisk power walk — so that it can work hard and more efficiently? If you want to know how healthy your heart is, you need to consider two factors: your heartbeat at rest and the tissue itself. First, heart tissue comes in three sizes.

Número Uno: A small and weak heart. When you do not exercise your precious heart, it begins to waste away and become weak, like any other muscle in your body.

Número Dos: An enlarged heart and unhealthy heart. These kinds of hearts are not very efficient, and it is when people start getting different heart diseases that these hearts work very hard to pump blood.

Número Tres: The conditioned heart. I **am** her fan!!! This heart is **healthy, strong, and** efficient. It works with less effort on each pump. It's strong and badass!

One of the best gifts that you can give your heart is physical activity. It is great to make your heart stronger, just like any muscle in your body. Your body will pump more blood with each beautiful beat. When I work out, I literally dedicate that time to my heart. I am so **happy** that it is working efficiently **every day**. With my clients, I always meditate at the end of each class. I always tell them to think about how happy their heart is for working out that day. It may sound silly, but it is true. Value all that your heart does for you; it is what keeps you alive, so take good care of it! When you understand the importance and value of your body, you will attach feelings to it, and then you are more likely to make a change. Take action not only for your outward physique, but for all of the great things that come with the amazing feeling of being healthy.

2. Respiratory System

> *"Why do lungs exist in pairs?"*
> *"Because they BE-LUNG to one another!"* -Sonali Gupta

This is another of my favourite functions of the body. It is one of my favourites because, as a kid, I used to suffer from asthma. It was pretty bad. I could not run or laugh too much, and in the wintertime, I needed to cover my body and my face because the cold air would often give me an asthma attack. It really sucked. As a kid, all I wanted to do was play with my friends. I remember when I went on vacation with my grandma and my cousins. We had a sleepover party. We were laughing our butts off, and because of that, I could not breathe. I remember my poor grandma going to my aunt's house in the middle of the night because I forgot my inhaler and my medicine. One of the things that the doctors suggested to my parents was physical activity like swimming, walking, and hiking. My parents listened, and as **I** grew up, my asthma went away. Physical activity will improve your lung capacity. The impact that aerobic fitness has on your body will exercise the muscles surrounding your lungs, and this will increase their strength and efficiency. You may be thinking, *this is fantastic, but what does it mean?* This will make your lungs more efficient organs, able to process more air and extract oxygen more efficiently. This will supply your blood with more oxygen. So now you know: exercise is not to just get skinny and grow muscles. Your internal muscles and organs will benefit, too.

3. Digestive System

> *"A good digestion turneth all to health."* -George Herbert

The digestive system is one of the most important and complex systems in the body. The body is so freaking smart. Your digestive system starts with your mouth and ends with the toilet. It includes your alimentary canal, gastrointestinal tract, and your gut. You consume food to survive, and your body (seemingly like magic!) breaks it down for you so that you can obtain the necessary energy to live and grow.

It is very important not to take for granted what you feed your body. It is easy to take your digestive system for granted, but it is so important to be aware of what you are feeding your body. Are you giving it empty calories that won't help with the optimal function of your organs and body? Or are you feeding it whole, nutrient-dense food that will help your organs and immune system? This is like anything in life: if you do not take care of the system, the system cannot take care of you. Whether it be a house, a car, a plane, or a boat, you name it — with time it will break down or some parts will get damaged.

In this case, however, we are talking about your *being* — your temple, what keeps you alive. Why would you not feed and take care of your most valuable treasure? Because you forget, you focus on other things, and you do not give it priority. It might be your paradigms and beliefs, but the good news is: now that your awareness is changing, you are taking control of your mind and your body. I recommend you ask yourself and answer honestly: Are you giving the best to your body? What can you do TODAY to help nurture your body? What excuses are you switching to an affirmation to break your old habits? Take action! Repeat after me: *"I have control of what I put in my body and how I nurture my body. I* **love** *the feeling of being healthy… it is amazing!"*

4. Brain / Mind

> *"The brain is wider than the sky."* -Emily Dickinson

As you might imagine, this is **my** absolute favourite. This is why I decided to write this book. The mind is one of the most complex miracles that God has given you in the whole world. Your mind is like having a superpower to create the healthy life that you've dreamed of.

The brain is an amazing three-pound organ that controls *all* of the functions of your **body**, interprets information from the outside world, and embodies the essence of the mind and soul. Your brain receives information from your five senses and assembles messages that give meaning to us.

Your mind has three basic functions: thoughts, feelings, and desires. Using your mind, you can imagine, perceive, think, judge, learn, and speak languages, and memorize anything you want. The difference between your mind and your brain is that the brain is an organ; it is tangible. Your mind is not an organ; it is intangible. The brain is the physical place where the mind resides. It is so important that you keep both healthy for the well-being of your health, and **for** the things that you want to attract and become.

You might be wondering, *how does exercise help my mind and my brain?* **What** a great question! Let's start with the brain. When you execute aerobic exercises, it increases your heart rate, and in turn pumps oxygen to the brain. This helps to release hormones that provide a great environment for the growth of brain cells. After an exercise session, you will feel happy and accomplished. I highly recommend doing it every day. The mind needs other types of exercise, too, however. There are many types of things that you can do to exercise your mind, like puzzles, using your senses, learning a new skill, reading books, challenging what you already know by learning different subjects, dancing your heart out, and keeping your mind motivated, inspired, and aware. Everything we have been studying in this book is a great exercise for your mind. Feed your mind positive, uplifting thoughts by repetition and positive self-talk. You will feel amazing, and your life will be better.

These are my favourite parts and functions of the body that make me value my beautiful being and my beautiful body. **It** is so important to understand all of the amazing things that your body does for you 24/7. Do not take your health for granted.

Taking care of your brain, your mind, and your body **can** help you prevent so many diseases in the future. Why wait until something bad happens to you or a family member to take your body and your health seriously? You are a freaking miracle, and God gave you the ability to live life to the fullest. It is up to you to take advantage of it.

I want you to close your eyes, take three deep breaths, and exhale. Did you do it? If not, do it now. Notice the beat of your heart, notice your chest going in and out. **Do** you feel the beautiful peace inside and out? Take this moment to acknowledge all the work your body does for you while you are sitting here reading this book, while you sleep, while you are driving, or while you are working. Amazing, right? Take a deep breath and thank your body for all that it does for you. Your body never lets you down no matter what you put it through. It is here for you. Say thank you, thank you, and thank you again. Make a promise to yourself and to your temple that you are going to take good care of it. You are going to feed it well, and you are going to move more, because it deserves to be taken care of on the outside, considering all that it does for you on the inside! It is time to give back to your body! It is time to take action. Feel it and say it: *I deserve to feel and look incredible!*

In the next chapter, we will be talking more about nutrition. Nutrition is the key to how your body will function, adapt, and behave. Food is what determines a massive piece of your overall health and the performance of your body. In the next chapter, I will be discussing how eating well is not a punishment but a perfect balance of health, for your mind and body. Eating well shouldn't be boring or strict — it should be a balanced, fun, and flavourful part of your life that you look forward to and enjoy.

Answer: I am healthy, strong, and happy every day. I love my body for what it can do.

Part 3:

Health is Wealth

"

Eating is a form of self-respect.

"

- Colleen Quigley

Chapter 7: Food is Memories

I strongly believe that food is memories. I grew up with delicious homemade food made from scratch, cooked by my mother, aunts, and grandparents. I learned the art of cooking from them. You really need to put passion, patience and *sazon*[17] into your cooking! All I knew back then was that food was good. Food was about sharing moments with family, happiness, tradition, and flavors. I never thought about what was healthy and what was not. I just wanted to enjoy time with family and bring delicious flavors to my mouth.

As time went by and I moved to the United States, I was immersed in a brand new and completely different culture. Food was different, and I was not surrounded by the same people, the same friends, or even my family. For the first time, I owned my food choices without any pressure. It may sound a little ridiculous to you, but think about it: you become what surrounds you. It is not only food, but the way you talk, the way you act, and everything else about you that is influenced by your environment. We learn these things as children based on what we see around us in our environments. I didn't notice anything strange or unusual about my environment — until I was in a new one.

Food is the most important part of your overall health. You become what you eat. Food will help your body perform well, give it nourishment in the form of vitamins, minerals, and nutrients, support the recovery of your muscles and systems in order to function properly, help satiate and satisfy you and your hunger, and, of course, it is an experience in taste, texture, and smell. A lot of people are misinformed about food and don't know the importance of it or what it can (and should!) be doing to support your body. We take it for granted, and we often eat what is most

---

[17]A Spanish word that states that a cook has the ability to cook things almost to perfection using the right time and the right spices.

convenient and what tastes the best without evaluating the ingredients or the nutrition that it has.

Now, I certainly am not telling you to only eat carrots and lettuce, but it is important to have a balance in which you give your body the nourishment that it needs, but also treat yourself once in a while. Food is like medicine; nutrients are nourishing substances that are essential for the growth, development, and maintenance of all beautiful bodies. When your body is low in nutrients, aspects of the function of your body will decline. Your cells and metabolic processes will be low or could even stop working. Thinking about food in this way does not even take into account the number of calories or grams it contains, and it really makes you think about and focus on the types of foods that we should include, rather than exclude.

I always tell my clients when they want a meal plan (because they want to lose weight) to focus on health, not weight loss specifically. You should love your body no matter what. If you love your body, no matter what shape it's in, why not love it even more by giving it the proper nutrients? Think about the long-term process. I always thought that because people get older, illness would come just from the simple fact of age. The truth is that all of those illnesses will come because of accumulated bad eating habits from not nourishing the body in the proper way. The old me would say, *"I am young; I'd better enjoy my life now while I can!"* or *"If I do not drink alcohol, my friends will think I am a weirdo."* or *"I am healthy now; I'd better eat what I want before old age comes."* All of those statements were paradigms and lies that I created for myself or leftover paradigms from friends and family. Food choices shouldn't be a punishment; they are habits that you slowly create. You can't just turn on a switch and say *"starting tomorrow I am eating healthy."* You need to take baby steps in order to have long-term success. And yes, you can still eat pizza or burger once in a while. It's called balance. You need to enjoy what you like. The key is to only do it periodically to keep your health in tip-top shape.

It is funny how we as humans know what our food weaknesses are. We even know it is bad for us, but we still keep eating what (according to us) it is impossible *not* to eat. That is bullsh*t. I am sorry, but it is. We talk ourselves into believing that. We are so attached to our culture or our family traditions that we refuse to choose a different way, or we believe the rest is not as good as a healthier way (or we are simply too lazy or too comfortable to make a change).

The sad part is that something will have to happen to our body or our health to make us want to take action. This is why I am so passionate about sharing and talking about health and fitness with people in my community. Health is not about your appearance; it is about nourishing your body and living a better quality of life. It is never too late to start. Take baby steps and decide to change your health *right now*. You know your weaknesses. Each week, eliminate a little something from your list. Add less sugar to your coffee, eat one less piece of dessert after dinner, eat a higher protein breakfast instead of a high carbohydrate one. You can improve every day. It doesn't matter how small your change is. Create new memories with food. If you have kids, show them a healthier way. If you don't have kids, lead and inspire others by example.

We seriously create a bond and a relationship with food. We generate a connection from the instant we look at it or talk about something we like or do not like. You can create good relationships with food. You may use it to make yourself feel better, to make someone else feel better, or even to show love to others. Or, on the opposite side, you can have a bad relationship with it like I used to. I used to think food was evil. I didn't want it because I thought it would make me fat, and every time it was time to eat, it was a painful sin that would affect my physique.

Food is one of the most sacred things that God and the universe gave you to survive and nurture your body. Food is an art. Food is here to take care of you and nourish you — if you eat it wisely. But food also can work against you. Nowadays technology and the "necessities" of human beings have changed. Food has been modified to last longer. Many foods are full of preservatives, and the food industry has created pre-packaged foods made with the sole purpose of having a long shelf life, marketed to us for profit. People eat more on the go and what is the easiest and most convenient. We do not take a minute to think about whether or not what we are eating is nourishing our bodies. We just eat when we feel it's convenient and tastes good, because our busy lives demand it.

In other cases, some people take care of their bodies with nourishing food, but the sad reality is — that is the minority. More people are getting sicker and dying younger than ever before, and their quality of life could have been greatly improved if they had paid attention to what they were consuming on a regular basis.

The good news is that you have control over what you put in your body. You just need to remember the importance and the *purpose* of food. Food will determine how you feel and how your body is going to function. You just need to pause, be aware, and recognize how you feel after eating something. This is a process if you are not into healthy meals yet, but it is an exciting process because once you make a **decision** to change your health, you will feel better and happier and you will never want to go back to your old self. In the next chapter we will learn how to start a healthier food journey so that you are able to experience — and stick with — better eating habits.

Remember, right now you have a current relationship with food, just like you have a relationship with a person. Just like every relationship can be improved, you can also change your relationship with food. You just need to have the will and the discipline to do it.

The most important part of all is understanding what food will do for your current health and your future health. In the next chapter, we will talk about how to start your food journey and how to stick with it. Healthy eating is a lifestyle, not a short-term goal just to lose weight.

Chapter 8: Your Food Journey

In my opinion, food is the most important part of health. We not only need food for obvious reasons — like, to survive — but we are also surrounded by it everywhere in our lives. Most of us have easy access to it, and we have many delicious options to choose from. The sad part is food has been altered and modified to taste better and to make it last longer, and it has not always been like that. Food companies add shelf-stabilizing chemical ingredients to their processed products so that they last for a very long time and don't get mold or "go bad." What they have not informed us about is that unfortunately, all of those ingredients are not good for human consumption. They are artificial additives, chemicals, and unhealthy ingredients that are not good for the body and overall health. The food industry hasn't been regulated very well, in my opinion. There are so many harmful ingredients in daily snacks, fruits, veggies, and meat, and we do not realize what we are eating. You might be thinking… *Okay, Deni...if almost all food is crap, then what the heck I am supposed to eat?*

The answer is easy. Try to eat whole foods, and if you are buying processed food, check your labels. The fewer ingredients there are in a food, the better. One-ingredient foods are ideal, and they often don't even have labels, so you can be sure they are good for you. Broccoli, carrots, apples — none of these whole and natural foods have a nutritional label. You can eat your favourite foods, but reduce them and eat them moderately. It is not about quitting your favourite meals and treats altogether. The problem comes when you eat foods that are processed, and filled with sugar or unnecessary ingredients.

This chapter will give you some valuable nuggets of information to start your food journey on the right foot. If you want to start eating healthy and want to stick with it, then you need to understand that this journey is exactly that: a **journey**. This is not a quick fix. Understand that you can decide to eat healthier because you really care about your health and your body. You can do this because you really want to feel more energized and have more vitality. You can, of course, go on a diet and lose some initial weight through restriction, but if you are doing this just to lose weight, you won't stick with it. You might gain the pounds back in the future.

You really need to feel and know the importance of what food will do for you, and why you need to start eating better. You must want to make the change for *yourself* first. Not for your doctor, your partner, or other family members. You need to be in charge of yourself and your choices in order to care for and protect what God and the universe gave you. You must want to feel in balance with your body and mind. You must truly care how food will impact your energy, your organs, your feelings, how you sleep, and how you live in this thing we call *life*.

If you don't really care about it and you just want to live the same way that you always have, not caring about how your life and your body will react in the future, then you won't be able to stick to a healthier meal plan. Most people are so attached to their paradigms, customs, and culture that they won't give it up even though they know it is not very healthy for them.

Many people will only change when something happens to their health, and they need a drastic change in their diet in order to shift things. I'm sharing these things with you because I want to show you how amazing your body and mind are. I want a healthier world with fewer illnesses and fewer mental health problems. A lot of the changes you want in your life when it comes to health can be shifted, adjusted, corrected, improved, or even solved with your diet.

I strongly believe that if more people knew the importance of movement, food, and mindfulness, that the world would be a better place. We just need to take responsibility for our own health, and the health of the little ones, by showing them a better way to live life using their mind and body to create a better and healthier world.

Once you've decided that you really want to do this, your food journey will be easier. Diets are not for you to feel sad or depressed because you can't eat all that you want. You should look at this like a new way to love your body and like a new relationship that you are going to start with food and your body. You should be excited and happy to feed and nourish your body with better food, nutrients, vitamins, and minerals that will allow it to work and function optimally. Your favourite foods can be eaten because everything is a balance. The first step is the will to do it and to know the importance of doing it. The next step is taking action. The key here is not to make a drastic change; take baby steps. Change your eating habits little by little, until you become the healthier person that you want to be.

Deep Breaths and Baby Steps

When I give a meal plan to a client, I make them fill out a 3-day diary of their food habits so I know what they like and what they don't like. This food diary usually shows me what can change immediately and what can stay the same way for a while. Usually, when people send me their diaries, they know what foods are not good for them, and they know what foods need to be changed. If you ask people the reason for their fitness/health goals they will answer immediately with the reasons why that they cannot be fit or healthy. As you know already, I call this response an excuse or paradigm. Recognizing and knowing why you do not do what you are supposed to do and eat the way that's optimal for you is a good thing because you need to start from there.

Pick one thing that you eat often, and that you also consider to be the unhealthiest. Take soda, for example. Soda is so popular it is like its own culture. In Mexico, people drink Coke as part of their meals every day, at almost every meal. If there isn't any Coke available, it is not uncommon for your mom or cousin to drive to a store until they find some. The obsession with soda drinks, including Coke, is also here in America. Reducing the amount of soda you drink could be one small change you make in your dietary choices. Pick one thing that you want to erase from your diet that you know is harming your health and your body.

Here is when you take a deep breath and take baby steps. Remember, you have to recognize that you are doing this to *nourish* your body. You are going to reduce the intake of whatever you pick. You won't eliminate it completely. Why? Because you won't be able to succeed on your new food journey if you try to approach everything with a "cold turkey" mentality. When you restrict yourself or forbid yourself from having your favourite things — the things that have become habitual in your life up until this point — you will instantly crave it. This is just a basic concept that all humans fall victim to. If I tell you **not** to think about a purple elephant wearing a blue hat, your brain immediately thinks about that image. If I tell you **not** to picture a stack of Oreo cookies on a white table…what image immediately shows up in your mind? It is not going to serve you to declare that you're never going to have an Oreo again if you've been having three cookies every night for the past 10 years. Start by reducing this habit to one cookie, instead of three, then maybe reduce your nightly cookie to just two or three nights a week. Then maybe you decide you'll have a cookie on Friday nights, but you'll try not to have any on other nights of the week (and if you happen to have one on a Wednesday when you weren't planning to, don't make a big deal about it). Don't make an all-or-nothing claim or decide that you will "never" eat something again. Not only will that be difficult to do, but you will feel terrible about yourself when you DO have the thing that you said you wouldn't have again, and you'll harbour feelings of guilt and lack of self-trust when you "cave" or "give in."

Let's not begin your journey to health that way. You need to take less each week until the necessity or the craving for it is gone. If you completely eliminate your favourite food, you will feel anxious, desperate, and angry — and you will crave it even more. It will be like the forbidden fruit, and you will end up going back to it. You'll feel bad about having it and perpetuate the low-level emotions and vibrations that are not congruent with growth in the direction that you want your mind and body to go. This first baby step is not easy, mis amigos. I get it, but this is why it is so important that you are doing this with the right frame of mind, so you do not feel like it is a punishment. Your body will feel an impact when you remove junk food, and it is better to do it in baby steps.

Removing *"No Bueno"* Food From Your Body

The human body is so miraculous. It is smart and does amazing things. When you start giving your body better and more nutrient-dense foods, your body will react and have some incredible changes. We are going to review some amazing things that will happen when you start making better food choices. It is like when you drink a refreshing thing when you are thirsty, or you take a shower when you are so sweaty. That amazing feeling of, *Oh yeah, I needed this.* Your body is going to feel the same way, and it will show it in many different ways.

Numero Uno: Weight Loss

I put this one at #1 because I wanted to clarify something. Weight loss is typically good (if you have excess weight on your frame), but I want you to see it as a secondary or "extra" gift that you

get for being healthy. Weight loss is a likely side effect you receive when you are making healthy changes to your lifestyle. You
should be focusing more on *why* you are making the changes,
though. You are doing it because you want to nourish your body
and have better health overall. But now that I have clarified that,
yes, you will probably release weight if you start making healthy
dietary choices compared to the poor ones you've been making
in the past, and you should be aware of how your food choices
can make a difference in your body composition (including potential weight loss).

The type of food you consume *matters*. Junk or processed food
has a much higher amount of things like salt, sugar, and potentially harmful chemicals, and they generally have more calories
without any added nutritional value. These are what we call
"empty calories." These are calories that provide no fuel or other
benefits to your body and can even be damaging to your health.
When you eat smarter — including whole foods in the proper portions — your body will be getting fewer calories by default. Let
me give you an example.

There are tons of "healthy snacks" out there, such as granola
bars. Usually, granola bars are promoted as a healthy snack, but
at the end of the day they are a processed food — and many of the
most popular "healthy" granola bars contain very high amounts
of sugar. Let's say you eat a strawberry grain bar. These "healthy"
snacks contain sugar, fats, syrups, oils, and chemicals that will
make them taste good and last longer, but will harm your beautiful body and make you hungrier. This is because it spikes your
glucose levels and eventually will make you crash. These tiny
bars will have approx 130 to 175 calories. If you are like me, you
need something more filling because if I'm hungry and eat something small I will end up eating more. When you eat whole foods
it is completely different. You can eat a full cup of strawberries or

a whole apple for fewer calories than those sugary granola bars. You will be providing your body with much higher nutrient-dense ingredients that will help your body perform and feel better. You will feel more full and less hungry. Why? Because you ate less processed, high sugar food — and a bigger portion of food. Your body will change when you put nutritious food into it. These whole foods will manage your hunger and keep you fuller with fewer empty calories.

Número Dos: You will have more nutrients in your body

When you eliminate junk food and give your body more whole foods, your body will have more space for better, more nutrient-dense food. Have you heard the saying "you are what you eat?" I will call it instead: "you are what your body absorbs from the food you eat." If you do not fuel your body with nutritious food, your organs, cells, muscles, brain, and even your mood will be crappy. You literally start digesting your food from the moment you smell or see food. Chewing your food and mixing it with acid (gastric juice) will start the absorption of it in your small intestine, and your amazing body will start the absorption process. All of these nutrients enter your bloodstream, which will carry proteins and bring nutrients into your cells. Your body is complex, and there is a lot going on when you put food into your body.

Your body, by default, does all of these miraculous things. All the food that you put into your body will be separated, broken down, and distributed to different parts in order to perform different functions. This is why it is so important that you fuel your body with nutritious food and not empty calories. It sounds logical, right? The better the fuel, the better you perform. But even though it sounds obvious, many people make poor food choices for various reasons. More and more people are getting different types of illnesses in increasing quantities around the world.

It is important that you provide your body with a variety of whole foods on a daily basis. Fill your plate with whole and colorful choices. This will help your body reduce the risk of damage to your physical health. You will have better sleep, more energy, your skin will look fabulous, and your organs will absolutely be doing happy dances every time you do this. The benefits of good nutrition go far beyond weight, *amigos*. This is about nourishing the most precious thing that God and the universe gave you.

These are the most important nutrients that your body absorbs in order to function well:

- *Protein* is essential for your body. Protein provides the literal building blocks of the body's makeup. Every cell in your muscles, skin, and hair has protein. It is used for growth and all of the maintenance that your body needs. You need to get these nutrients from food because your body cannot produce all of the essential protein that you need.

- *Carbohydrates* are also essential nutrients. They fuel your body, brain, and, according to research by the Mayo[18] Clinic,[18] protect you from disease. Carbs get a bad rap, but the important thing is to eat *complex* carbohydrates that are high in fiber. These carbohydrate sources will come mostly in the form of vegetables and fruits and are not to be confused with the empty carbohydrates from *"no bueno"* foods like white bread, pasta, and the like.

- *Fats* also have a bad reputation. I used to think that they were the Devil. Healthy fats are essential because they support a lot of the body's functions and help aid in nutrient absorption. Fats help you balance blood sugar, are anti-inflammatory, and are so easy to find in nuts, coconut oil, avocado, or seeds.

---

[18] Mayo Clinic
https://www.mayoclinic.org/healthy-lifestyle/nutrition-and-healthy-eating/in-depth/carbohydrates/art-20045705

- *Vitamins* — Your body needs these goodies for proper function. Each vitamin plays a different role in the body, and when you do not get enough, guess what happens? Yep, you get health problems or diseases. Vitamins are essential for healthy vision, skin, and bones.

- *Minerals*, just like vitamins, give support to your body. They will help your bones, teeth, and even your metabolism.

Now that you know how important it is to fuel your body with these nutrients, imagine what might happen when you eat the *"no bueno"* food — empty calories with zero nutrients. Your body will slowly deteriorate, and in the future it will affect your health.

Número Tres: **You will have more energy.**

Fast food usually has more salt and sugar than most food. Lots of "healthy" food, however, also has tons of sugar. A serving of salad dressing, for example, can have 4-12 grams of sugar, along with tomato sauces and other popular condiments. All of these ingredients are hiding in plain sight on the nutrition label, and you often do not notice them when you eat processed food. When you eat sugar, the pancreas will start working. It will secrete insulin to keep your blood sugar low. But because fast food doesn't contain enough complex carbs to give you long-lasting energy, your blood sugar will crash right after you finish eating, leaving you tired and with lots of cravings to eat more sugar — causing another spike/crash. When you stop eating junk and fast food, you will feel better and have more energy, because you won't be dealing with these constant blood sugar fluctuations.

Número Cuatro: **You will be in a better mood.**

It has been proven that sugary and unhealthy meals affect brain behavior. Harvard conducted a study[19] and found that women who consumed more junk food such as soft drinks, refined carbs,

---

[19] https://www.health.harvard.edu/blog/gut-feelings-how-food-affects-your-mood-2018120715548

processed meat, and margarine triggered inflammation and had a higher risk of depression compared to women who ate healthier food. This is a good reason to eat better if you want to improve your brain and your mood. The gut, or microbiome, in the body determines not only your mood but your overall health as well. There is a really good book you can read about gut health. It is called *Brain Maker* by Dr. David Perlmutter, and it explains how mental health depends on the various microorganisms that live in the body. These bacteria will eat what you feed your body, and they affect your immune system function, inflammation, and many other important factors in the body. The microbiome affects your mood and even your perception of the world. Crazy, right? I'm telling you… the body is a freaking miracle, and if we give it love and good stuff it will perform better and you'll be healthier.

Número Cinco:
You will improve your memory and your ability to learn.
I do not need to tell you that junk food will affect your brain and mood. You might know this already, but do you know how or why? When you eat junk food, the circuits in your brain activate and release a chemical called dopamine. With repeated exposure, your brain can become overwhelmed or addicted to this rewarding food. It will adapt and create more receptors for dopamine. Some side effects of dopamine addiction include feeling depressed, impatient, addicted to sugar, vulnerable, anxious, hyperactive, or even dementia. According to a Harvard study[20] diets high in cholesterol and fat might speed up the formation of some type of plaques in the brain. These plaques will cluster and damage the brain. There are lots of other studies that show that eating a poor diet is not only bad for your overall health, but also for your brain's health. There are specific foods that will help your brain thrive. Just pick healthy, whole foods to promote your overall health.

[20] https://www.health.harvard.edu/mind-and-mood/boost-your-memory-by-eating-right

Número seis: **Fewer food cravings**

When you start feeding your body with quality, nutrient-dense food, your cravings for junk food will naturally decrease. This will allow you to opt for healthy food rather than less healthy food. This is setting you up for long-term weight management and health success. Remember how we just talked about gut bacteria? By gradually eating better food, these bacteria will stabilize your blood sugar levels, which will help your cravings and your taste buds will adapt to the healthier food as well. I can give you a very clear example: When you have a package of your favourite cookies and you say, "I'm only going to eat one cookie," what happens? You end up eating more! This happens for various reasons, but from the gut bacteria perspective, these bacteria will crave sugar if you do not feed them healthier food. You want to eat healthy food every day so that the microorganisms in your gut become addicted to these ingredients.

Número siete. **You can eat more food without gaining weight.**

I need to tell you that this is my favourite one. When people see my plate they say, "goodness gracious, are you eating all of that?" When I eat, I need to see a rich, full plate. If my meal is a granola bar or a bag of chips (usually junk food), I will end up eating more food and, subsequently, more calories. Junk food has so many calories and is full of bad carbs and sugars. A large meal of whole foods will give you the same amount of calories and all of the macronutrients that you need, leaving you satisfied for a longer period of time. Your blood sugar levels will be balanced, and you won't crash and feel hungry again in a short period of time.

Mis amigos, food is medicine, but who doesn't like junk food? I love ice cream, cookies, and the like, but I choose to eat them only once in a while because I need to enjoy life. It is impossible to avoid food indulgences completely. You travel, you go to parties, you have holidays, you have social lives. You would go crazy avoiding it every day unless you have strong willpower and you build up a habit of avoiding junk food, but this absolutely takes time.

My goal in writing this book is to show you how amazing your body is and to tell you that the more you nourish it, the better quality of life you will have. If you are like me and don't like to go to the doctor's office often, want to have better skin, live longer, lower your blood pressure, play with your kids or grandkids without getting tired, or simply be happier, energetic, and with more vitality, nourishing the most precious thing you have is your best bet. We may all have different relationships with food, but all it takes is dedication, willpower, and a simple understanding to help you overall.

I challenge you to start today (yes, today), not tomorrow. Pick one thing that you are going to improve, and remember that baby steps are important. Within a week of giving your body better food, you will start noticing amazing side effects. Use your journal and write down any changes that you feel in bullet points. Your energy levels will rise, you will sleep like a freaking baby, your bloating will decrease, and you will feel more empowered, confident, and energetic. Hell yeah, who doesn't want that? The answer to your prayers is within you. There is no magic pill, machine, or shake that will "fix" your problems. They may mask them temporarily, but food and movement will do so much more for your health and body.

My honest answer when people ask me which is more important between exercise and food is always food. You can exercise and have an amazing physique, but if you're eating *"no bueno"* foods, your body internally won't be as healthy. Good food will maintain a healthy weight and will make your body perform better. Exercise is the art of stressing your body and making a change in your physique. Exercise will absolutely benefit your heart, your muscles, and your overall body, but food is the key to optimal health.

In the next chapter, I am going to introduce what exercise does for your body and why it is important to stay active. Exercise is another passion of mine. That is why, after studying for an engineering career, I decided to become a personal trainer. Exercise is what helped me get away from my eating disorders. Exercise held my hand and made me feel good. Exercise changed my body and my mind. Exercise literally taught me that withholding food and hurting my body that way wasn't okay. I needed to eat in order to exercise. Exercise liberated my mind and made me feel indestructible. It made me happier and more confident.

In the next chapter, I am going to share all of the benefits of exercise with you, and I am going to show you why you should move your body every day. I want you to fall in love with the art of exercise, because if I can convince you of the amazing things that will happen to your health and body, you will inspire people around you to live healthier, which will create a domino effect — inspiring more and more people to do the same. My goal is for the world to become a healthier place, with less illness and pain.

"

Exercise is an art where you connect with your body and your mind... where your body expresses itself with power and strength.

"

- Tdachi-Deni Whiting

Chapter 9: Move Your Body

What is Exercise?

Currently, we are bombarded with the news that we need to exercise. We see commercials and our social media is full of fitness ads. It is great advice, but it is sad at the same time. It means that we are moving less. In our current world, everything is more convenient. We do not need to catch our food. Now we can just order food from our couch. We take our car to go places, we watch more TV, we sit for 8 hours at work. Unfortunately, our current lifestyle makes everything easy and convenient for us. Believe me, I love the convenience, but you need to remember that your body is designed to move.

Moving your body is vital for your mental health, your strength, your skin and your organs. Moving your body gets your heart pumping and makes your blood flow more efficiently. Blood carries oxygen and nutrients to "worker cells" throughout your body, including your beautiful skin.

Exercise is an art. I call it "art" because it is a connection between the mind and body in which you can perform crazy things and shape your body in different manners. I am forever grateful for my Greek fellas for inventing physical activities back in ancient times.

Exercise is basically a physical activity that is planned, structured, and repetitive that will improve your health and maintain fitness. There are many types of exercise out there, so explore what movement feels good and works for you and your body. Exercising regularly and staying on a plan is one of the biggest challenges that I've seen with my clients. They will start the first day excited and motivated and a month later they will be giving me a million excuses why they can't do it anymore. It all comes back to your paradigms and the *"no bueno"* self-talk you give yourself daily, convincing yourself that you have better things to do than moving your body. Now you have the tools to shift those paradigms and that crazy bad talk you give yourself. It is time to tell yourself that you will move your body for all of the benefits you are going to receive when you do it.

You've probably heard this before in many posts and quotes: Exercise is a celebration of what your body can do. Your body is designed to do amazing things. Take advantage of it. When you don't exercise or move your body, your muscles weaken and lose bulk, including the muscles you need to breathe. Without regular exercise, over time you will become more breathless doing everyday activities, and simple movement will make you tired. Not exercising or moving enough is a confirmed risk factor for premature death. Sedentarism has been causing the most deaths around the world in recent decades — even more than cigarettes and alcohol. How sad is that? The good news is that you as an individual have the power to change that if you change your habits and have the desire to improve your health.

The relationship between our bodies and movement has largely been forgotten in our society today. We only notice our bodies when something "goes wrong" with them. Unfortunately, this is often the time when people will decide to make a change in their life. Why wait until your body breaks down? Do not ignore the most beautiful thing that you have. You are the lucky one that made it. You exist. Honor your life by living as fully and healthily as you can.

Movement and Exercise

I absolutely love the phrase, "Exercise is optional; movement is essential." You might be wondering, *Deni, what is the difference?* Exercise is like a painful, *"no bueno"* feeling for some people — an obligation or chore. It is often the case that once people decide or even think about doing exercise, their vibration is low because they don't want to do it. Movement is different. Movement is ancient and has been here since man appeared on this planet. Hunting and gathering, dancing around a fire, walking, running, jumping, crawling, climbing, lifting, swimming, fighting... these are all movements that the human body uses and is capable of doing. Current research tells us that we need to move more; "sitting is the new smoking" as some research has shown.[21] Movement in your life is *essential*, and exercise is an optional, extra "medal" that you can add to your life. You can live your whole life in perfect health even if you move without going to the gym. If you just focus on moving your body instead of constantly sitting, you can absolutely remain healthy.

As I mentioned before in another chapter, you need to find something that inspires you and makes you *want* to move. Find out what movement means to you! For most, moving is being in the present, enjoying the moment — like going for a walk, playing golf, swimming on the beach, or cruising on a bicycle. The more you move your body, the better it is going to get at moving. The less you move your body, the harder it will be to move once you decide to start.

It doesn't matter what way you choose to move. Remember, it has to be something that you absolutely love to do — or at least want to try — because if it isn't, you won't stick to it. Exercise and movement have to be on your daily schedule. It has to become a habit, like taking a shower or brushing your teeth. Your body will love you and perform better when you do this on a daily basis.

---

[21] https://www.startstanding.org/sitting-new-smoking/#extended

Leading a more active lifestyle takes time, effort, and determination, but in the end, it's really worth a shot. Here's what will happen to your body when you start to exercise regularly.

When You Choose To Exercise Your Body

When you decide to join the gym or an exercise class, this is what will happen: If you haven't been active in a while, you might feel like your heart wants to come out of your chest when you are doing your first workout. Maybe you won't be able to do it for a long period of time and you will have to take breaks. That's okay! It is completely normal to feel this way. You are a freaking winner because you took your first step. You are a winner because you are not doing something else, and you decided to take care of yourself and your beautiful body. During that first workout, you might feel more alert and energized because ramping up your heart rate means a boost in overall blood flow and oxygen to the brain. But prepare yourself for the day after — you are going to be sore and sitting on the couch or the toilet might be a little difficult for you! The soreness is completely normal and lasts approximately two days, but the good news is that you're less likely to be sore again as long as you continue to regularly exercise those same muscles.

Over the next few weeks, you will start feeling the great effects of exercise. You will feel more confident, energized, and happier. Your body will be saying *hell yeah, move me, baby, let's do this.* The molecules in your body will be doing happy dances inside of you, and all of the slow processes that your body uses to function will become faster and faster. The endorphins in your body will make you feel amazing, and your stress level will begin to decrease.

After six to eight weeks of regular exercise, studies have shown that people can increase their mitochondria by up to 50%.[22] With

---

[22] https://www.businessinsider.com/benefits-of-regular-exercise-2018-1#:~:text=After%20six%20to%20eight%20weeks,did%20during%20that%20first%20week.

more mitochondria in your cells, you'll start to feel more fit and your endurance will increase, so exercise will no longer feel as difficult as it did during that first week. A few months later, all of that hard work should finally start to show. If your workouts focus on strength training, you'll notice your muscles begin to take shape. Your jeans will feel looser, you will see muscle definition, and you will absolutely be so confident and happy with what you have accomplished.

When you just keep training as part of your daily life, you will become a complete badass and feel like the healthiest you. You're going to live longer than you otherwise would have — and that longer life will likely feel more fulfilling, more productive, and, most likely, you will do things that you didn't want to do before.

This is how exercise changed my life. I was trapped in my eating disorder, thinking that I could be skinnier by not feeding my body. In reality, the only thing I was doing was harming my precious body and shortening my life. You can't just quit exercising or movement. Do not expect fast results, and don't do it just for "looks." Focus on a long-term goal and the whole package you are going to gain by moving and exercising your body.

The majority of people know the advantages of this and still do not move or exercise. It is a paradigm shift that you have to commit to and a self-talk that you need to have with yourself, otherwise there will never be a change.

Now you know how to do this. Affirmations, shifting your self-image, and journaling are the tools that you need to use to reprogram your mind and start living a new lifestyle, acting in a different way so that you can make better choices. Use this book as a reminder that I will always be here to be your cheerleader, but 90% of the responsibility is yours. Only *you* can make this shift. Is it easy? NO, absolutely not. Nothing that is worth it is easy. You need persistence, faith, and discipline. The best part is that we are talking about your life and the most valuable things that you have in your existence: your health and your body.

In the next chapter, we are going to talk about mindfulness. The mind is another very important part of health. Without a healthy mind, we cannot be happy and healthy, and life would be very crappy. It is so important to work on our powerful mind, so come with me while we learn more about how to take care of it.

"

Your body hears what your mind says.

"

- Naomi Judd

Chapter 10:
Mindfulness and the Body

This is my favourite part of the book. I truly believe that the mind is the one thing that is going to unlock everything you want in your life — not only healthwise, but the mind controls how you perform, react, and live life. It is not very common to hear that you need to take care of your mind, your thoughts, your stress level, or your self-talk. If the mind isn't in the right place, it can impact the body in a negative way. If you have a healthy mind, your body and overall health will be in tip-top shape.

Your brain and body are connected through neural pathways made up of neurotransmitters, different chemicals and hormones in your body. These magnificent miracles control your everyday functions, including ones that you don't even think of. Your digestive system, your pain, your thinking, your feelings (if you feel anxious, depressed, etc.) are all controlled by the mind.

I never paid attention to the power of my mind, especially when I was a teenager, until my body couldn't handle my craziness of not eating well and collapsed. That was the time when people told my parents, "maybe she needs to go to a psychologist; she needs help." It wasn't until I was scared of disappearing from this planet because of the stupid stuff I was doing that I realized my mind was the cause of all the mess. It was my paradigm. Paradigms literally control your logic and your behavior. I used my mind to get me through my problem by being positive and reprogramming the self-image I had about myself. Even when I was putting it into practice I had no clue what I was doing until a later age, when I got into personal development and started studying some books. I realized that I used my mind to get out of my crazy old Deni paradigm. Lots of people do this without realizing it just because they need to make a change and have no other choice.

My point and my reason for writing this book is to show you that you don't have to get to that "breakdown" situation in order to make a change in your life, no matter what it is. I think it is so important that people take the time to take care of their minds. When you do that, you will literally become a powerful being. I used to think this kind of thinking was "hippie stuff" and that my mind was perfectly sane, but I started to pay attention to how I could change my state of mind just with positive thinking or cheering myself on. I noticed that by simply playing my favourite music, my mood would switch and I would be in a better mood. You are in control of your emotions, and you are in control of how you control stress.

Nowadays people are more disconnected from their beings. We live busy lives; we are always in a rush; we have smartphones, social media, and most likely all we do is by habit.

If you examine yourself you might have the same routine in the mornings. You turn off your alarm, check your Facebook, your email, post a picture of your coffee in the morning and then take a shower and go to work. You are not even thinking about how you feel and what is in your mind. Or maybe you are already pissed off because someone didn't like your post on Facebook or someone left a mean comment on your post. Your emotions are set from the moment you wake up, and everything you do, read, or tell to yourself will define the rest of your day. Lots of people might say "I woke up on the wrong side of the bed," but they do not realize that they are creating that outcome.

You can change your state of mind by giving yourself a talk or by being aware of your thoughts and emotions. When you are aware of this, you have the power to decide if something is going to affect you or not, and if you are going to internalize that thought or that comment and let it influence your mood. When you start working on your mind and connecting with your body, you won't get affected by little things. You will be more focused on your happiness and well-being.

I used to think and repeat to myself things that bothered me. For example, if an ex cheated on me, I would be unhappy for three months, hating that person and just poisoning my body and mind with negative thoughts — and that was all my own fault. I decided to internalize that memory over and over and over, and each time my body would be so mad. My stress levels would go through the roof and I would be in such a bad mood just for the simple reason that I kept thinking about the same thing over and over.

It is like a Telenovela (a novela is a latin serial drama soap). Man, they are dramatic! When people watch that, they take it so seriously. If the main character cheated on the wife or if the bad guy is about to burn a house, viewers will internalize it and feel the emotion. They will yell at the TV and say, "Be careful, do not go to the house! The bad guys are about to burn the house!" It is the same when we watch a movie. In my case, I will probably be crying in the movie theater, because I internalize the moment and my emotions get involved.

It is the same with your thoughts. You can change your emotions and your body's state by listening, watching, or thinking about the right stuff (or the bad stuff). What I am trying to explain here is that you must *choose* the positive emotions that will benefit your body and mind the most. You can create and be whatever the heck you want! You are so powerful and don't need to fill your head with bad thoughts, habits, and negative self-talk. You should go on the internet and look up Joe Dispenza. He regenerated his body with his mind by using meditation.

You would be amazed at how powerful your mind is. You can make yourself sick by thinking and filling your mind with crap, or you can create the healthy, prosperous life that you want. You might think this is guru stuff or maybe you have heard of it, but have never really had to sit and work on yourself. I am telling you that **you are a freaking miracle!** You can do and create amazing things if you just believe and put effort into it.

In the next chapter, we are going to go more in-depth about how your mind works and why you have the health that you currently have, but most importantly we are going to review the steps you need to do to keep on track and get the results that you want. At the end of this chapter, I will have a little surprise for you. Let's keep going and dig deep into this.

The Power of Your Thoughts and Your Words

"The most important words you will ever hear are the words you say to yourself, while the most important opinion is your own." -Marissa Peer

Your thoughts are powerful and mystical. A thought can be an idea, a sound, an image, or an emotion. Your thoughts are electrical signals that propagate by millions of neurons. Your thoughts are your energy. Your words are energy. Your actions are energy. You will manifest your thoughts and words by the end of this journey. Look around you and examine yourself. Everything that you have in your life is the result of your past thoughts, self-talk, and words that you speak out loud. When I started taking personal development seriously, I started reading books and meeting successful people. I was like, *holy crap, why doesn't the whole world know this?* Why aren't we teaching this in school? The world would be happier, healthier, and wealthier if that were the case.

The reality is that the majority of people live their life without knowing this, thinking their life and their results are because of bad luck, and that successful, healthy people are just different than they are. Others think this is just "hippie stuff" and never open their hearts to study more about the topic. Still others just settle and are too lazy to challenge themselves or to take the time to live a better, healthier life.

I look back at my life when I had no idea about all the power of being. It was like a vicious cycle. My life had limited purpose. I lived unhappily, and I sometimes used alcohol to produce perceived happiness. I was just living, not thriving. I never looked beyond my present or created bigger dreams for myself, either, because of criticism or fear of what other people might think. My self-talk was nasty. I lowered my self-esteem, sabotaged myself for eating food, and punished my body. The results of all of that craziness weren't good at all. My health was *"no bueno"* until the point that my body couldn't take it anymore.

There is a silver lining, though! Bad thoughts, jealousy, fear, telling yourself you can't do things, anxiety, and more — can be cured and your body and mind can be in calmness and happiness if you only shift your thinking. The same happens with your health. You may keep telling yourself all the stuff you can't do, or *"no bueno"* thoughts like "I can't stop drinking soda" or "I need my Cheetos when I watch TV," and focus on those beliefs or paradigms. Another example is that you might be so scared of getting a specific illness, or maybe you have a specific illness and you focus on the negative aspects instead of thinking in a positive way. If you concentrate your energy on the negative and become a victim, you might not see any progress in getting healthier. Everything you think will become a part of your physical reality. If your thoughts are negative, more negativity will come. If your thoughts are positive, more positivity will come into your life.

Keep your mind alert and you will start noticing all of the thoughts you have on a daily basis. You will notice that all you are and all you have is because you put it on repeat every day. You will catch a glimpse of the superpower that every single human being has. You, me, and your neighbor have this power.

It sounds crazy, right? It is so crazy that many people don't believe in it and never apply it. It is not easy to reprogram the mind. People won't persist. People will give up even knowing the power of their minds. They will come back to their old self for lack of persistence and desire. It is more comfortable to stay the way you are instead of putting yourself to work to better your life and mind. Now I am asking you: Now that you know you have the power to change your health and your life, are you going to put in the work? Are you ready to reprogram your mind so you feel happier, healthier, more vibrant, less anxious, and stress-free? I need you to have the desire to say *"Hell yeah! I am ready to freaking change my life!"*

There is an amazing woman called Marissa Peer. She is an author and Hypnotherapist. She is amazing and I actually did one of her programs. I needed to reprogram myself. My issue was that I didn't give myself enough time to relax. I couldn't give time to myself because I thought it was a waste of time. I needed to be productive. My mind was always working, thinking ahead. I wasn't present. I didn't sleep much because all I wanted was to be productive and I was so strict with myself. I attended one hypnotherapy session, and I reprogrammed myself with audio. Remember, it takes at least 21 days for your brain to change its old way of thinking. This is the most amazing thing that I've done for myself. Now that I enjoy life more, I know that it is okay to leave some things pending. Now I am more present for myself and my family. My past was creating this disruption in my present mind. Past events made me think and believe that I needed to be productive and perfect all the time. Anyone can do this and reprogram their current image. All you need is determination, persistence, and a burning desire to change whatever you want to change. It won't work if you start doing it for five days and then stop.

Nowadays the media, and even doctors, remind us how important being thin is when it comes to being healthy. Yet, we are also bombarded with food. This food is not best for us, and it is cheaper and more accessible to us but has harmful ingredients. Society is confused, and that is why it's important to take control of your mind and your thoughts. You need to eat smarter, not less. You need to learn how to program your mind and change your current habits forever, not just to lose weight in the short term. You need to identify what is making you eat more or less. It might be the way your family educates you about food or even the influences of your friends. In my house growing up, I couldn't leave my plate full. I could not waste food, so I ate all of my plate and would even finish somebody else's food so it wouldn't go in the trash. Later, I prohibited myself from eating because I thought food was the Devil and would make me fat. You need to track and attack all those silly thoughts and words. You need to give your mind better instructions of what you want. Your mind will do what it thinks you want. If you keep telling yourself that you can't stop eating chocolate, for example, you need to change your thoughts to I choose not to eat chocolate because *I will nourish my body with nutritious food.* You need to put this into practice from the time you wake up, to when you put food on your plate, and until you go to sleep. It is all practice and later it will become an automatic mindset. Your choices will be healthy by default when you put this into practice.

Decide, take loving action, and don't quit.

When you decide to become a healthier version of yourself, think about the words "loving yourself." When I was asked that once, I thought, *what do you mean? I love myself* — and I got offended. I want you to think of it this way instead: Ask yourself the question, "What can I do to take care of my beautiful self?" This way you are opening your heart, you are ready to learn, and you will include your feelings as you start this beautiful journey that literally will change your health and your life. When you put your feelings into anything you do in life, you are going to have more success. You are going to fall in love with the process, and you will have a spiritual connection between your mind and your body.

When you make the decision to start this process, your fears, beliefs, experiences, and doubts will be put to the test. You might have heard all of this information about the power of the mind before, but if you are completely new to the subject, you might have fear or doubt about it. This is real — this information is based on the laws of the universe. God created you to be happy, healthy, and the best version of yourself that you can be. You have to analyze your current life. All you have and all you are is what your thoughts were in the past. You might have an "a-ha!" moment and suddenly realize that you have infinite power and can create the healthy person you want to be. The hardest part is to keep working on yourself. Lots of people get access to this information but will abandon the journey later. They will start working on themselves and somehow will again convince themselves that this is a waste of time by using their old paradigms. Believe me, it is so tempting to take the easy route. It is easy to live the way you are living and make no change. Many people would rather take the easy route because of fear or overwhelm. This is why it is so important that you work on your self-image and cheer yourself on every day.

There are some steps that you can follow to take action and keep your heart and soul persistent. Evaluate yourself, be honest with yourself, and take that honest evaluation to literally attack your weaknesses. You can do this. Anyone can! You just have to have willpower. Let's review some points that you need to consider and evaluate about your beautiful self to be successful in this journey of building your new **Power Health Self.**

Número Uno: **You must have a *desire* to change your health**
It's not just a desire, but an energy that comes from the inside — a feeling of excitement, a feeling that says, *I cannot freaking wait to start doing this for myself.* It's a goal that is connected to your feelings and will not let you quit even if everybody else is telling you to quit. You need to have a beautiful "why" that will keep you on track.

Número Dos: **Willpower**
Willpower needs practice, and this is the only thing that will keep you on track to do all that you need to do to get to your health goals. You build willpower like a muscle. You work every day at getting your willpower stronger, by doing little things that get you closer to your goals. Start with achievable goals that will strengthen your willpower, like getting support from others, getting into health groups, following healthy pages, or exercise groups to help you stay on track.

Número Tres: **Discipline**
If you just say to yourself, *Oh, man… I am not very disciplined,* then that is the first thing you need to change in your self-image script. You HAVE to change this paradigm. Write down "I am so proud of myself because I follow through on my commitments." or "I am so happy and grateful that I am so disciplined with my workout routines."

Discipline is key in this process. You need to put work in on yourself for at least 21 days. You need to show up for yourself. If you are lacking in this step, change your thoughts and your words to reflect the new habits you are practicing.

Número Cuatro: **Be your own cheerleader**

Be honest: Do you cheer yourself on, or are you a Negative Nancy, telling yourself how you can't do certain things? If your answer is the latter, that is your second most important step. You need to be caring and kind to your own beautiful self. You are so powerful and amazing and need to understand that. You need to understand that you need *yourself* to get through anything in life. You are a miracle, and you need to talk to yourself like you are motivating your best friend.

Número Cinco: **Stop being a victim**

Start a new day and start a new you. Stop being a victim. Stop using old excuses as to why you can't do something. Stop blaming circumstances or people for stopping you from your goals. Let it go. Start a new you. No one is responsible for your life except you.

Número Seis: **Criticism**

Stop caring what other people might think of this new you. You need to stop worrying and putting your dreams on hold because of what people might think of you. People might not understand because they are living their own paradigms, and that is okay. If you already made that decision, shake it off and stay focused.

Número Siete: **Create experiences**

Experiences will give you the most powerful tools on this journey. You are going to grow your willpower and your persistence by doing what makes you healthier. By moving, by eating better food, and by taking care of your thoughts and your words, you will feel empowered and start noticing changes in your life. Make sure you create experiences.

These steps will give you a firm foundation on this journey and will keep you on track to achieve your goals. Evaluate yourself and see what you are lacking, and use that to write your self-image script. You will absolutely know what you need to work on.

Everybody knows their weaknesses. The problem is that we never work on them, and today is the perfect day to start. In the next chapter, we will review all the steps you need to take to be successful on your new Power Health journey. These lists will guide you and keep you on track so that you can succeed in this process.

It is important that you are always honest with yourself. Do not procrastinate. When you start seeing that you are going back to your old self, come back even stronger. Tell your ugly paradigms, *Hell no, I am not going back! This is my new me, and I choose to show up and better myself and my health.* You won't be the only one that will have these thoughts of failure and giving up. Every single human being has a lack of persistence. It is a muscle that every single person has to exercise so it becomes part of them. It has to become a habit, like brushing your teeth or taking a shower. You are on this planet for a very short time. Why not live a healthier, happier, and more meaningful life by using your mind and the beautiful laws of the universe?

Let's review in the next chapter how to be a winner on this journey. I will give you a handy synopsis of how to start working on your new **Power Health Self**. You are going to love the process because your idea of health will change. You are going to fall in love with your amazing body and automatically want to nourish it with better food, less alcohol, and other harmful things. You will feel happier and less stressed and anxious when you try to be healthy, because now being healthy is not just about losing weight. Being healthy is so much more than that. When you fall in love with your amazing and precious body, the rest will automatically come.

"

Everything is hard,
before it is easy.

"

- Johann Wolfgang von Goethe

The Final Steps

This is it! You are one step closer to starting on your new Power Health Self. I already gave you some tools that will help you understand different aspects of health. Health has different meanings for each individual. Everybody will look at health differently, and that is okay. Your main focus should be on the whole body, physically and mentally. You have to understand that you are so lucky to be here on Planet Earth. God, the universe, or whatever you believe in gave you the breath of life. The human body is a miracle. It is so smart and it is what keeps you alive. You are here for a reason. You have a purpose. You are here breathing and enjoying the amazing things in life. You can create beautiful experiences with no pain, anxiety, or sadness. You have the power to create the life that you want with your thoughts and your mind. Feel lucky and blessed that you have the opportunity to live, to give, to love, to laugh, and to cry. Use your powerful body and gifts to give, to love, and to make an impact in other humans' lives. Leave your print on Planet Earth with something that you love.

You are amazing, you are worthy, and you deserve to live the happy healthy life that you want. Your beautiful self has the power to do it. It is up to you to create what you want. Most people will never get this information or take the time to read or learn more than they know. Most people just "live" doing and thinking the same things until the day they die. You are a step ahead. You might know this information already, or maybe you are just finding out. Use this information. Feel lucky for having access to it. Feel grateful for your body that keeps you alive every single day. Now is the time to give back. It is time to give God or whatever you believe created you their gift back. But now, do it bigger and better. Let's give back a healthier and happier life — a life that will help people, love people, and inspire people. When your mind and body feel healthy… *mis amigos*, you will be freaking unstoppable. Nothing and no one will stop you, and guess what? You are in control of that. You can start whenever you want and it will cost you *nada*, zero.

You can read this book and say "Oh, it was cool" or "This is a fairy tale" and keep living the same life you are living now. Or, you can take a deep breath and say "Today is the day! I am doing this ayayayayay!" And you can start right away — it is your choice. No one else will change your life. Only you! Do not wait like I did to take action until I was so freaking scared for my health. No, do *not* wait until it gets worse! Do not wait until that bad or scary event happens to change your mind and make a change. Do it NOW!

I am writing this chapter now at my parents' house in Mexico. So many memories come to my mind when I visit here. The old me and the new me. The girl who wanted to be like other girls or celebrities. The girl who punished herself and was so hard on herself with thoughts and words. The girl who thought she needed to be skinny to fit in at school. The girl who had no clue what health meant and starved herself, not knowing that she was harming her body. The girl who wanted a pretty body without any movement. The girl who was anxious and unhappy all the time. The girl who was so focused on herself and did not pay attention to the people she loved. The girl who needed to have a scary event happen with her health to wake up and make a change.

I honestly typed this and felt sorry for my old self because the only person responsible for that was me, and no one else. That is why I am writing this book… because maybe you are reading this book and feeling the same way. Or maybe it is something else. You might be focusing only on your weight. Maybe your mind is not at ease or maybe you just want to feel better. It doesn't matter what it is. You have the power to change your state of mind and literally transform your body into a healthy body. The doctor won't do it. He might give you a temporary fix. Pills will mask whatever it is, or maybe in the future might make things worse, and that will punch you in your pretty face and spur you to make a change. It might sound a little harsh, but this is why I am here sharing this with you. I don't want that happening to you. I am here to support you so that you make that change. I want you to feel amazing, happy, loved, calm, energetic, and full of peace. If I can change my harmful thinking and use the power of my mind to get the health that I want, then you can too. Use this powerful information as many others have. You can also do it!

I know you will do it, because you are reading this book and that desire is there. You have already done the hardest part. Now the next step is to put it into practice. Is it easy? Nope, it requires work, discipline, and persistence. But seriously, when something is worth it, it won't be easy. You need to go through the process, because the process will make you stronger and teach you so many different things.

You only live once. Close your eyes and just be aware of the simple fact that being alive and breathing is the greatest gift that you can receive. Love your body and love every single part of it, inside and out. Taking care of your body is your most precious treasure while you exist on Planet Earth. Nourish it, pamper it, and feed it nutritiously so that every single part of your body gains vitality, nutrients, and can work and perform better. Love the fact that you are unique and there is no one like you. Be original, be yourself, and do not try to look like anybody else. Use your soul, your body, your mind, and your uniqueness to inspire people, to love, to give, and to live your life to the fullest.

You are a powerful being, capable of creating and doing anything you want if you put your focus on it. Do not let people tell you what you have to be or how you have to look. Do not live life just to live life. Move, laugh, jump, and celebrate, because each minute that passes is one less minute you have to enjoy life.

My soul is on fire right now. I am just full of gratitude because I know how to use my inner self to create the health that I want. I am so excited that you are going to put all of this into practice and start building a new, healthier you. Now you know that health is not all about looks. Health is a balance between body and mind. Health is being free of illness, free of pain, and free of stress and anxiety. Now you know why all of those habits and thoughts that you have are the result of your culture, your parents, your friends, and your inner self-talk. Now you know that you have a self-image that can be changed by repetition. Now you know how to become the healthy person you want to be. You just need to work on your mind.

My Power Health Self: Memorandum

"This is a memorandum to remind myself that I was created in God's image. I am a miracle and I am unique. There is no one like me. I am blessed for being alive and for being me. I am grateful for every breath that I take and for the wonderful things that my body does for me. I am grateful for my heart that started beating since I was in my mother's womb. I am grateful for every beat, every cell, and every organ that allows my body to perform well and to keep me alive. I am grateful for my five senses that allow me to experience and live in the present.

I am grateful I can see all of the wonderful things on Planet Earth. I am grateful for every hug that I can feel and every kiss that I can give to my loved ones. I am grateful that I can smell and taste different foods, plants, and fruits. Thank you, body, for being unique and for every single part that makes me… me. Thank you, body, for all that you do for me every day, every minute, and every second. Every breath that I take, I realize how lucky I am to be alive. I do not take for granted the simple fact that I exist and have the opportunity to be me and to share my love and gifts in this life.

My body and my being are enough. I am enough and I nourish myself with nutritious food. My body deserves to be nourished because I deserve to be and feel healthy, energetic, and happy. I move my body because it was designed to do amazing things… to run, explore, climb mountains, and put my toes on a sandy beach. God and the universe provide me with amazing things to enjoy and to accomplish my wildest dreams if I just focus and put my energy on it. I am a powerful being full of love and excitement to live a happy and healthy life.

Nothing and no one can tell me how I have to look or feel. I have the power to LET GO of hurtful words. I always look to the positive in things and forgive. My mental health is important and because of that I keep myself healthy, positive, and active. I am my biggest cheerleader and I keep my thoughts positive, encouraging, and faithful. Now I know — what I think, I attract — and because of that, I vibrate and manifest all that I want. I am here NOW and I am fully responsible for my well-being and my beautiful body. Today I take proper action to be the best version of myself, because I deserve to feel and look incredible."

Get the audio of this Memorandum here!

Epilogue

As a personal trainer, I wanted to write this book to encourage people to look at health from another point of view. We live in a very graphic and modern world, where we have access to media from all around the globe. We have access to great information, but some of that information can confuse us and make us feel overwhelmed.

The Internet was just coming out when I was little, and access to social media came much later. I did not have access to different diets, celebrity pictures, and millions of exercise programs at my fingertips. I felt confused and had no idea what health meant or about the power of my mind. Now we have access to too much information, and that can make us overwhelmed. We want to look like girls on Instagram and eat the same diet as Kim Kardashian, thinking our butt and waist will look the same, when the truth is that everybody is different and every body will adapt to different food and portions. I hope that this book opened your mind to approach health in a different way, and helped you approach becoming healthier from a different place, other than losing weight.

Losing weight and being at a healthy weight is important for your health, but that will come with a whole package when you learn how to love your body and feed your body the right food. When you start your journey to become healthier from your heart and from wanting to nourish your body, you will realize *holy crap, I look slimmer!* Every single one of us will have different goals. Some people want to have abs, but some people don't care about abs. Some people want big muscles and some people think big muscles are silly. My point here is that everybody has different goals and different ways of being healthy. There are so many different ways to move your body; there are so many different kinds of diets; and there are so many ways to take care of your body. I do not criticize any of them, because as humans we are all different and everybody has their own likes and dislikes. What you should consider when you are trying to be healthier is thinking about how to move, feed, and spoil your beautiful body in the best ways that you can, so that it performs optimally.

Now you know that everything starts from the mind. Our thoughts become our ideas, and our ideas become our habits. Our habits become us. So if you keep telling yourself all of these bad, negative thoughts and make excuses, you will remain the same or you will be on your health journey for a very short time. You need to change your habits and your thinking by repetition so it can all stay stuck in your brain. You do this by repetition and by auto suggestion to all of your bad habits that do not let you reach your goals.

A healthy lifestyle is the composition of many good habits, and you need to start working on them one by one and little by little. These will become part of you, and when you look back at all of these little efforts that you made, you will literally be a new person with a new Power Health Self. You will feel better and won't automatically crave bad foods, and you will want to move your body by default. It won't be so hard to be healthy anymore. Why? Because it will become ingrained in you. It will become a habit like brushing your teeth or taking a shower. This is a process. It doesn't take a week or two, but a little short-term progress is what will keep you going while working on your mind. You only live once. You just have one opportunity to be *you*, and to be here on this beautiful planet. You are so lucky to be here now. You deserve to live life to the fullest. No one is better or worse than you. No one has more privileges or more luck than you. You are a human being, and you have the same power as other human beings. You just have to focus your thinking so that you start changing your body and your mind. You need to open your mind and believe that you are a freaking miracle and that you have so much to give.

Please forget about the excuses you started with or the attitude you have about health. Learn to know your beautiful self. Learn and communicate with your thoughts and your body. Value the fact that you are here reading this book while your heart, cells, and organs are working to keep you alive without you noticing all of the amazing stuff happening inside of you.

Kiss yourself in the morning if no one does. Look in the mirror and promise yourself that you will take action and that you will start caring for your body *today.* No more ugly and harsh words toward yourself. You deserve to feel and look perfect in your own favourite way. You exist for a reason; be grateful, give love, and inspire others. Be aware of your thoughts, what you tell yourself, how you react to things, and how you make excuses for yourself. Put in the work for you. Work on your paradigms. It is free! You just need to repeat the right words and thoughts to yourself and everything will fall into place. Live life to the fullest, not just to survive. Don't wait to live life when you get old. Value the time you have on Planet Earth and enjoy life in a healthy way. You are a powerful being that can create and manifest all of your craziest desires, if only you take action to work with yourself — and your mind.

About the Author

Tdachi-Deni is a Mexican entrepreneur who discovered and unleashed her life's purpose while studying abroad and traveling to the United States in 2010. Tdachi-Deni has a degree in Industrial Engineering, but later in life discovered her passion for helping others in the health and wellness industry. She is now a successful certified Personal Trainer, Thought Leader, and Life Coach who is on a mission to improve her clients' minds and bodies internationally!

When she isn't teaching fitness, inspiring her community, or studying mindset and health topics, Tdachi-Deni enjoys spending time with her husband and son in their hometown of Tampa, Florida. Her goal is to help as many people as she can to unleash the power within their souls so that they can attract the highest level of health and wellness that they deserve. She truly believes that the world will be a better, happier, and healthier place when they discover some of the concepts and ideas featured inside *Mindset for Health.*

Recommended Additional Reading and Resources

1. Psycho-Cybernetics by Maxwell Maltz
2. Thinking Into Results (online/mentored study program)
3. I Am Enough by Marissa Peer
4. Think and Grow Rich by Napoleon Hill
5. Fitness: The Complete Guide by Frederick C. Hatfield, PhD
6. The Joe Rogan Experience (health related)
7. Mindvalley app / Youtube
8. Jay Shetty
9. Dr. Joe Dispenza podcast

What Now!?

For more information about Tdachi-Deni Whiting, and instant access to exclusive health and mindset bonuses and resources, scan the code below!

Testimonials

"Being married to Deni gives me a behind-the-scenes look at the work and dedication she puts into each one of her clients and her craft. She spends countless hours researching, implementing, testing, and sharing these tools/ideas which are getting absolutely incredible results! I couldn't be more proud of her, all of her clients that are getting these results, and her future clients that will absolutely fall in love with her and her process!"

—Layton Whiting,
Wesley Chapel, FL, USA

"While training with Deni, I learned how to fuel my body correctly to avoid cravings and energy crashes. I also got in the best shape I have ever been in! Her upbeat attitude is what makes it so fun."

—Jessie Westhoff,
Guttenberg, IA, USA

"I love that I can get an amazing workout in the comfort of my home. Deni has been incredibly supportive and motivating. I love that she does the workout with you. I indeed have seen amazing results. I feel confident and sexy. She is a Godsend for my physical well-being. "

—Trishan Govender,
KwaZulu Natal, Durban, SA

"Deni helped me to trust in my inner power to do what I set out to do. Thanks to her guide, now I love exercising. I am learning to eat healthier and in a balanced way. It also showed me the world of meditation which has greatly favored my life. It helped me guide my thoughts towards the positive to receive everything with gratitude. She has definitely changed the course of my life and I am very grateful for her."

—**Gaby Martínez,**
Ixtepec, Oaxaca, México

"Deni is an amazing coach who has helped me want to work at being healthy. With her guidance, I am exercising, eating better, and enjoying a more positive life. Thank you, Deni!"

—**Maggy Simonsen,**
Wesley Chapel, FL, USA

"Deni helped me say goodbye to my anxiety. She helped me feel like a confident empowered woman and know that everything I set out to do, I can achieve. She has created a healthier routine in my life, eating better, thanking my body, and taking care of it. Since I started exercising with her, I see life from another perspective, from gratitude and happiness. Thank you, Deni, for being my guide and my inspiration. "

—**Nidia Guadalupe Martínez Jacome,**
Puebla, Pue, Méxic

"Working with Deni has been amazing. I was able to continue PT exercises at home and get back to where I needed to be. She was able to modify certain exercises that worked my hip, knees, and ankle to still gain strength and still be a part of the group/team zooms. Grateful to have her as a coach and mentor! "

—**Jared Wessels,**
Farley, IA, USA

"Deni has helped me to have more confidence in myself, eat healthier and the most important thing to me, is that I no longer eat because of anxiety. I reduced sugar consumption for me and my family.

Thank you very much Deni, you are light, strength and guide in my life. I am very grateful to God and to life for having put you in my path."

**—Alma Rey,
Monterrey Nuevo León, México**

"I am so grateful to the great human being that is my coach Tdachi-Deni Whiting. My life took a radical change both physically and mentally by initiating a change of habits with her. Her passion and love helped me to change a lot of bad habits with food that I had. I feel stronger, healthier, and filled with peace and happiness. Now I think about myself, my health, my goals, and my overall sense of well-being. Thank you, because with everything you teach me, I have achieved the greatest gift of being a mother.

Thank you, you are the best!"

**—Ingrid Dianet Solis Figueroa,
Veracruz, Ver, México**

"I am happy to have met Tdachi because seeing how she takes care of herself and eats healthy has motivated me to change my eating habits, to exercise and take care of my body. I love her super positive and upbeat attitude."

**—Yuli Lara Gomez
Toronto, CA**

"Deni brings energy and excitement and love to everything she does! She guided me on my journey to heathier eating and exercise, and through her training I lost 14 pounds, and loved every minute of it with her. Her passion and commitment inspire me to always continue towards my goals. I am truly grateful to have her as my trainer and my friend!"

—**Michele Puco**
Bradenton, FL, USA

"Getting to know you changed my life inside and out. You complement the spirit with the body. You helped me know that I can do it. Thank you for showing us the way with love and dedication, showing that you love what you do. "

—**Alma Rosa Cruz.**
Xalapa Veracruz, México

"I had thrown in the towel having tried over and over again to start physical activities. In short, I couldn't find the needed support in the gyms and at-home the activities had no end. The pandemic did not help and by the end of 2020 I saw that I had gained a great amount of weight. Anxiety in that particular year was very difficult to handle at home and my refuge was food. I started classes on a Monday with my friend, who always with her words and cheers made me feel that I could do things. I had been doing absolutely nothing for years, but Deni injected into me the desire that I had already thrown away, she always encouraged me to give more than I gave in each class. I started changes in my daily routine and I discovered the things I could do, at first, I couldn't even jump. Deni was undoubtedly a watershed in my life, she helped me to overcome my fears, to regain the confidence that I had lost in myself and above all to promote, apart from exercise, other activities such as meditation that have helped me a lot to control my anxiety. Deni changed my life, not just mine, that of many more people together with whom we form a beautiful community full of support and motivation. I learned things that I did not know I was capable of and am so thankful for your support."

**—Sandra Basurto,
Xalapa, Veracruz Mexico.**

"Deni's program helped me to change my habits, to be more aware of the importance of my physical and mental health. Thanks to her, my food decisions are healthier, and I stay more active during the day."

**—Ximena Ridgeway
University Park, MD, USA**

"I loved working with Deni on my fitness and nutrition journal. Her program was tailored to me and my needs. Her program focuses on good habits, mindset, and individual goals. She provided me with the right tools to keep going. Deni is very professional, with a positive attitude, and challenges you to become the best version of you!"

**—Omarys Soto
Wesley Chapel, FL, USA**

"I've lost 20lbs, added strength, flexibility, and more endurance. I have greater physical strength than I've had in years, and a number of minor pains, primarily in my back and knees, have gone away completely."

**—Yaritza Aimee Jimenez
Wesley Chapel, FL, USA**

"I have known Deni for a while already, and I always see her thrive in everything she does. She inspired me to join her in the fitness world and it definitely changed my life. She guided me to make the right decision for my life, to challenge myself to become the best version of me. Her nutritional facts and tips were very helpful as well as her workout routines. She walked me through every single step along the way. I never thought I could achieve everything I did. Thanks, Deni, for all that beautiful energy you spread all over. "

—**Natalia Wood,**
Northern Virginia, USA

"Deni is an amazing human being. She's a genuine person, her self-less way to share and help others amazes me. I am so glad we crossed paths, she was one of the people who introduce me for the first time to powerful concepts such as mindset, visualization and more to reach my goals and manifest my higher self. Concepts that I use today and every day to keep my balance in life."

—**Dacia Verdugo,**
Washington, DC, USA

To find out more about LeadHer™ Publishing,
including how to publish your own project
or join a group co-authored project,
visit www.lead-her.com.

Other books available from

LEAD-HER.COM